Holy Ground

Holy Ground

© Jyoti Sahi 1998

This book is copyright
No reproduction without permission
All rights reserved.

Published June 1998 by:
Pace Publishing
P.O. Box 15-774
Auckland 1007
New Zealand.

Fax: 64-9 817 35 74
Email: pace@iconz.co.nz

in association with:
The Asian Christian Art Association
Kyoto, Japan.

Printed by Clearcut Printing Co. Ltd. Hong Kong
Photos by Jyoti Sahi unless otherwise credited.

ISBN: 0-9583632-0-X

Holy Ground

A New Approach to the Mission of the Church in India

Jyoti Sahi

This book is dedicated to

Father James Tombeur S.A.M.
who in his enthusiasm
for Indian art and
architecture
in the context of the Indian Church
has been a great inspiration.

Contents

Foreword - Masao Takenaka 7
Acknowledgements 9
Introduction 11

1. Early Syrian Churches in Kerala 19
2. Colonialism and the Church 37
3. Orientalism - Shadows of the Past 53
4. The Missionary and the Local Church 75
5. The Ashram and Architecture 91
6. Church Building as Teaching Aid 111
7. The Prayer Room 125
8. The Church as a Seat of Power 139
9. Tribal and Dalit Churches 159
10. Holy Ground 179

Glossary 189
Bibliography 192
Index 195

Foreword

On behalf of the Asian Christian Art Association (ACAA), it is a great joy for me to celebrate the publication of this book by Jyoti Sahi. *Holy Ground* is timely and provocative. It is timely because many church leaders are thinking today about the appropriate style and form of contemporary church buildings. It is also provocative because the author raises challenging questions which relate the church building to the mission of the church in the world.

I have known Jyoti Sahi since the first consultation on Asian Christian Art held in Bali Island in 1978. At the end of this conference ACAA was created and Jyoti became one of the founding members. He has contributed immensely to the development of the ACAA not only through his participation in meetings and exhibitions but especially though his creative work in writing and paintings.

I believe Jyoti has a unique gift in creative writing which is seen especially in works such as *The Child and the Serpent* (1980) and *Stepping Stones* (1986). These two are outstanding works in the field of Christian art in Asia.

There are some significant points about *Holy Ground*. It is the first book to probe deeply into the history of church building within the context of Indian mission. In 1995 I edited the book, *The Place Where God Dwells - An introduction to Church Architecture in Asia*. This book was meant to be just an introductory survey of the subject in Asia and I had hoped to see significant works dealing with a specific country. Jyoti's book fulfils the hopes I had at that time.

In addition the balanced historical survey which Jyoti presents in the first part of the book is followed by a study of the functional use of the church building from a missiological perspective. He raises significant questions about the way buildings in India have been used for the mission of the church in community. It is most important for both artists and architects to consider not only the aesthetic form of the church but also to think how it will function to serve the people in and around the church.

Thirdly, Jyoti focuses our attention on some of the frontier issues including the challenges of Dalit and Tribal cultures and their relation to the Indian church. In the light of new cultural sensitivities what are the lessons we learn from those cultural traditions in India which increasingly reject Hindu culture?

These questions are of utmost important, not just for the Indian churches, but also for many Asian churches as we enter the 21st century. Through his creative style of writing and with vivid illustrations, Jyoti Sahi has pointed us in a new direction so that we can express the Christian message through the traditional cultural gifts of the people.

Masao Takenaka,
Honorary President
Asian Christian Art Association

Acknowledgements

This book is the fruit of 30 years involvement in the field of designing for the Indian church. I have dedicated this book to the memory of Father Tombeur but of course there are many others in those early days who were a great influence. Dom Bede Griffiths at Kurisumala Ashram, architect Laurie Baker living nearby and Mathew Lederle who died tragically in 1986.

Fr Amalorapavadas at the Catechetical Centre in Bangalore and Fr Jacob Theckanath who was always a great friend and supporter. Cecil Hargreaves whose book on 25 Indian churches was the foundation for this present book.

The Asian Christian Art Association through Dr Masao Takenaka and the Jesuits in Nuremburg, through Fr Ubelmesser both provided grants which assisted the research for this book.

Ms Caroline MacKenzie and Mr Paul Middleton together helped to arrange the exhibition of Indian churches commissioned by the National Centre which was the basis for the small book Adisthana which led in turn to the publication of Holy Ground.

Many other people contributed to this book including Fr Claude d'Souza in Bangalore, Dr K.M George, Fr Jacob Thekkeparampil, Air Cmdre and Mrs A.W. Chakko, Dr George Oomen and Dr Ram

Guha, Bishop Patrick of Varanasi, Mgr Malenfant, Fr Ishwar Prasad, Rev Brian Lee, Brother Arul and numerous others.

I am profoundly indebted to the support of my family. During the period of preparation for this book my father was in the slow process of dying and much of my writing was done at his bedside. He has always supported my artistic work and gave me insights into his Hindu roots which could not be found in any book.

Special thanks to my wife Jane who has always worked with me in each stage of preparing this book. My daughter Lavanya is studying to be an architect and we visited many churches together and my son Kiran helped with taking photos.

Finally I express my sincere gratitude to my editor Ms Alison O'Grady who has patiently followed this work over the last two years through many revisions. Without her editorial skills this book would not have taken the form it now has.

Jyoti Sahi
Art Ashram, March 1998

Introduction

In 1967 I left my job teaching art and went to Kurisumala Ashram, having been invited to go there by Fr. Bede Griffiths and also by Laurie Baker who was then living near the Ashram. It was in the home of Laurie Baker that I first met Fr. James Tombeur. He had come to see Laurie in connection with some designs for fishermen's houses to be built in Muttom, not far from Kanya Kumari. He invited me to visit this village on the coast where he was working to set up a co-operative for fisherfolk. It was then that I saw the small group of churches in Kottar district which he had been instrumental in building. I was fascinated by the idea of building a church drawing inspiration from a Hindu temple. Fr. James asked me if I would design a set of Stations of the Cross for the Parakunnu Church. Later, I made a mosaic for another of his churches and began plans for other works. That was one of my first commissions to decorate the interior of an Indian church (James Tombeur, "Lead by God's Hand" pub Nalini Nayak 1990).

Over the last thirty years I have been working for many different Churches all over India. In 1977, after settling down in a Christian Dalit village north of Bangalore, where I had come to work for the National Biblical Liturgical and Catechetical Centre, I was invited to attend a meeting in Bali, Indonesia, of Asian Christian artists. That was another significant milestone in my life. It is important to have these milestones, because then one has reference points which provide a kind of structure to one's personal journey. Through the Asian Christian Art Association, which was officially founded in 1978, I became aware of the wider Asian situation with regard to the church and the place of art in mission.

In 1983 Fr Mathew Lederle encouraged me to start an art ashram in the village where my wife and I had settled down to live more than ten years earlier. He suggested there should be a place where young artists could live in an ashram setting and learn through practical involvement in actual commission work about the need in the Indian church for visual forms which would express an underlying Indian theology.

In 1992, when I was still involved in the cathedral at Varanasi various events led to the destruction of the Babri Masjid in Ayodhya. That was a great shock to me. I just managed to get back to Bangalore a day before the final demolition took place and the whole atmosphere was extremely tense. After the actual destruction of the mosque, riots broke out. The worst violence was in Ahmedabad and in Bombay, which I had passed through only a few hours earlier on my way home. Following these events, I felt the whole spiritual landscape of India had changed. India had traditionally been a pluralistic society in which temple, mosque, church and folk shrine stood side by side giving a distinctive character to village or city. Now, almost overnight, we began to sense that these buildings no longer represent a harmonious fabric of creative interaction but stand in conflict as built manifestations of dividing walls.

About that time we began collecting information about different Indian churches, many of which I had known personally and reflecting on the efforts to create an Indian Christian architecture.

In 1993 the National Biblical Liturgical and Catechetical Centre in Bangalore celebrated twenty-five years of its work and for this occasion Fr. Michael Amalados gave a series of lectures on "Fullness" in memory of the late Fr. Amalorpavadas who had been the Centre's first director (Michael Amaladoss S.J. "Towards Fullness" NBCLC, 1994). On that occasion, the art ashram in which I was involved held an exhibition of photographs showing some of the attempts to make an Indian style of church in different parts of the country (Jyoti Sahi and Paul Middleton, "Adisthana: Sacred Space" pub NBCLC, Bangalore 1993).

Enthusiasm for an Indian type of Church and discovering the richness of the Indian artistic heritage, which was very much alive in the Church in the 1960s, has changed a great deal and is apparently a spent force. There seems to have been a growing sense within the Indian church over the past fourteen years that other concerns have priority. Development and modernisation, along with a concern for liberation from the suffering of grinding poverty and injustice have been the focus for the most creative thinkers within the Church. The ashrams themselves were challenged by the question: what were they doing to change the plight of the suffering masses? Were contemplation, spirituality, an interest in symbols or art mere luxuries? Both the monk and the artist have had to justify their existence by showing that they possessed a deep underlying concern for humanity even in a life of prayer and the search for beauty (Vandana Mataji, ed. "Christian Ashrams - a Movement with a Future?" ISPCK, Delhi, 1993). The blind forces of prejudice and violence, which erupt when a sort of fundamentalist tunnel vision cuts out of sight all those wider concerns which characterise a truly human concern for the world in which we live, threaten justice and peace far more perilously than any lack of material resources. I am often confronted with the reaction: "But you need so much money for art, and architecture! How can these resources be spared when there is so much poverty around?"

Do art and poetry, architecture and music have to be seen as luxuries, meant only for a leisured elite? Villagers and tribal communities have produced a rich culture out of the simplest means. Strangely enough, it is the very ashrams which have emphasised the relationship of true culture and spirituality to a simple style of life and encouraged the reduction of material wants, which are now being rejected as irrelevant in a world which now seems to believe in economic growth and expenditure to the exclusion of all other human values.

Globalisation is taking hold of India, as we become swept into a monetary system over which individual nations no longer have much control. Wants and economic growth become the order of the day and anything which questions the ultimate value for humanity of such a market-oriented society is brushed aside as being utopian and impractical in the worst sort of way.

Unless the people have a vision, a sense of community will die. Perhaps never before has that been truer than today. Fifty years ago, at the time of India's independence, there was a vision. How much of that vision is left? Essentially, this book is about that vision, about what it meant and will continue to mean for the church in India. There is much talk about "Evangelisation 2000". It is as though an old millenial dream has come to replace the faith that nothing significant can happen in salvation history, which does not concern itself with the now, with the everyday. Simply trying to convert more and more people to the church in poverty-stricken Asia while in the affluent nations of the west more and more people are leaving the church, is not going to bring the *eschaton* (culmination of all things). What is needed urgently is a deeper reflection on the many different ways in which God has been revealed to different peoples all over the world. As we come to a greater understanding of the diversity and complexity within human cultures, we should have a new sense of awe before the mystery of divine revelation. Perhaps art has a way of looking into the future which is not available to the rational or scientific mind.

Revelation is like a seed, often hidden in the soil. The person who plants the seed does not know which seeds will germinate, or even where they have been planted. Seeds, like ideas, apparently disappear. But suddenly they emerge again, bringing the promise of a new future.

Somewhere in the effort to find an Indian cultural form to the gospel there lie the seeds of a future visioning. The field has been prepared, often with much labour. Who knows what fruits all this will bring in the future? I believe that the harvest we are looking for is not just a matter of drawing everything within the church but rather respecting and nurturing the rich diversity of forms which we find abounding in all cultures. We are now in serious danger of losing this diversity.

The study of Church architecture which has given rise to this book has emerged from two concerns. First, there is the historical problem, which relates to the way in which cultures have evolved and interacted with each other. How does a community develop a sense of identity and how does culture play a role in political events such as, for example, the process of domination which we call colonialism and the emergence of liberative movements which give rise to nation building? The church has to engage itself in the political world, as that is part of what we mean by inculturation. The church cannot remain on another plane of reality, claiming to have no dealings with ordinary human affairs. The church enters into history and as a result takes certain historical options. When Christianity came to India alongside colonial forces it was fulfilling, however unconsciously, a political role. Later, when the Church realised that national aspirations were an important aspect of liberation, then again inculturation took on, quite clearly, social and political overtones.

The second part of this book addresses the problem of incarnation at another level. The theology of inculturation arises out of a belief in the incarnation. True religion is not something which affects the mind or the spirit alone. The body, and all that the body implies in the sense of physical awareness and the use of the senses, also constitutes an essential aspect of being human and fully alive.

The church as a built space is an extension of the body. If the body is not taken into account, then providing it with shelter becomes spiritually meaningless and architecture is unnecessary in the context of true worship. Where a religious spirituality rejects the physical body and focuses only on the spiritual or mental aspects of the human faculties, the church or temple as a built form also loses its significance.

The church building reflects not only an attitude towards the body but also serves the process of sacramentalising the body. The church building is even understood as the body of Christ. The built form helps the worshipper to discover a new dimension of being present in the body and ultimately finding the Lord enshrined within the "cave of the heart". All sacred architecture ultimately points back to the incarnation of God into the physical being of the worshipper. In a way, the building serves as a door through which divine reality is experienced as entering first into the cosmos, and then through the cosmos and nature as we experience it with our bodily senses into the very heart and physical self-awareness of the worshipper. The external form of the building, its use of materials, its sacralising of space and time, intensifies the senses of the worshipper, so that ultimately God is experienced as incarnated into the life and physical being of the worshipper.

This process of discovering the spiritual reality of God incarnated into the physical and tangible world which we experience with our senses is the basis for what we call liturgy. Liturgy is not just something which engages our intellectual faculties. Liturgy involves the whole body and our physical contact with fellow beings. That is why the liturgy has provided the matrix within which the built form is sustained and nourished.

The continued practice of a ritualised form of worship gives permanence to an architectural tradition, be it the building of a church, a mosque or a temple. The reason we can speak of a Syrian type of church building, is not because of any social institution which has consciously developed and supported any particular style of building but rather a continued tradition of worship, using symbols which have their roots far back in antiquity. It is the Syrian liturgy which has given rise to that form of building which we can identify as being typical of the Syrian Church.

But liturgies, or rituals and sacraments, do change (Michael Amaladoss, "Do Sacraments Change?" TPI, Bangalore 1979). The sacrament is not once and for all - it is itself a response to social and cultural conditioning, even though it also represents the power of the eternal in transforming and renewing individual lives. When we talk about the sacrament of baptism or marriage, or the eucharist, there remains a constant understanding of what these terms imply, theologically speaking, but the way in which they are performed varies from culture to culture.

This sacramental aspect of the church as building is the main concern in the second part of this book. The church has itself been understood as a sacrament. Where should Indians worship God? Worship is not just something performed within a church or temple - worship is a way of understanding the whole of life. As an artist I have often stressed that being creative, the way in which the imagination is used, is itself our way of worshipping God - what in Indian spiritual tradition is called the individual's *sadhana*. (devotional path or search). When, as human beings, we believe that we were made in the image of God, this does not mean that we picture God having arms and legs like we have. That would be making God in our own image - which is, unfortunately, what we too often do. Rather, by believing that we are made in the image of God, we affirm that our imagination is itself a divine gift, a means which has been given to each person, so that everyone can receive a divine revelation. God is revealed to us through our images. It is with this understanding that this book attempts to describe the form of an Indian church.

The crucified Lord as the Sanyassi (monk).
Chapel of the Medical Mission in Bangalore
(Jyoti Sahi)

1

Early Syrian Christian Churches in Kerala

There is a kind of veil which hides the early art and architecture of the Syrian Christian Church in Kerala. This is partly because of the very troubled history of the church in Asia, and in particular in south India. The early Aramaic Church, the church which had its basis in the first Semitic community of disciples around Jesus, was very much alive in the first centuries of the Christian Era but later it was overshadowed. This ancient church was arguably the very source of an understanding of mission received directly from the ministry of Jesus himself. However, the initiative for evangelisation largely passed over to the Greco-Roman branch of the church, partly because of the achievements of the apostles Peter and Paul.

Perhaps we forget too easily that the early church spread far and wide into Asia, to Babylon and Persia, to the shores of India and even further to China. This movement eastwards was later to encounter many difficulties. It was a comparatively poor and powerless church with none of the patronage which was afforded later to the western church by the all powerful Roman empire. Soon this eastern branch of the church was deeply divided by theological debate, not helped by the fact that theology soon became one of the instruments of political manipulation and was used to marginalise those seen to be insufficiently subservient in matters related to the craft of states. For the last two thousand years Asia has been struggling against the powerful principalities which have had their thrones in the west. First it was Rome and Greece which held sway but later the tide of trade and military power shifted to the emerging nations of Europe and colonisation extended the influence of an empire centred in the west.

Despite this, the Asian genius continued to exert a creative influence which often was not properly heard, partly because it was not clearly, or at least understandably, articulated from a western point of view. For example, we still hear it said that Asia, from which many of the great religions of the world arose, has contributed little to the theological thought of the church. In part this is because the paradigms which determine theological discourse in the west have never taken cognisance of eastern patterns of thought. The same ethno-centricity which tends to marginalise whole civilisations is, even today, to be observed in books about art and architecture which take serious note only of concepts of beauty and creative forms developed in the west, beginning with the Greeks. Indian art and architecture, not to mention the vast cultures of China, North and South-East Asia, are often put into parenthesis and seen as "interesting" but hardly significant for the future of what is vaguely termed "modern art". Even the term "globalisation", which is so often used today, assumes that it is western culture, or more properly the culture of the north, which will dominate.

The purpose of this study is to look at the built forms and images found in the eastern church, with particular reference to India, as an attempt to see theology in a different way: as something not just to be understood through rational and discursive thought but as arising out of ways of doing and celebrating life through signs and symbols. An attempt will be made to relate the building to liturgy and narratives which have given shape to local cultures. The building should not be seen outside the context of the whole life of the community for whom the church serves as a focus. Perhaps this approach will account for a special stress on the "mystery" dimension of belief: that ultimately speaking, what we live through faith cannot adequately be described in words.

The church, as it took root on Indian soil, had to accommodate and live alongside a plurality of faith expressions - Hindu, Jain, Buddhist and later, Islam - in a way that the western church rarely had to do. This in itself helped to form a profoundly theological stance which engaged much of the energies of the early church in Asia. It was easy for the western church, married to a mono-cultural system of polity characterised by the Roman empire, to be exclusivist. In an increasingly pluralistic world, the church is now realising that it cannot simply claim all truth for itself. It has to come to terms with the fact that many other religious traditions have had their share of revelation. But the fact that eastern churches had to come to terms with the truth statements to be found in other religious systems of thought laid them open to the accusation of being "syncretic", of compromising somehow the one unique truth which is to be found in the gospels and of being drawn into the web of Gnosticism.

The Asian church had to struggle profoundly, and in the lived context of this vast ocean of plurality of cultures, with the mystery of incarnation and the insertion of gospel within culture. There is a danger in talking about gospel and culture in dualistic terms which, in fact, denies the incarnation by suggesting that faith and culture are two mutually exclusive dimensions which somehow have to coexist in this imperfect world of dichotomies. It could be argued that faith can be articulated, and therefore discovered, only in and through culture because culture is as much a part of our spiritual experience as the body is part of the soul. This would mean that we can speak only of gospel/culture as we speak of time/space, recognising that the gospel itself is found in and through different cultures. We do not have one standardised gospel which somehow survives the human plurality of many cultures. Even in the Bible the church has accepted four gospels, each of which views the life and ministry of Jesus from a different cultural perspective.

The problem is that this stress on an incarnation theology

seems to work counter to the concept of mission which has so often characterised the church, wedded as it is to political and cultural imperialism. When missionaries started accompanying soldiers and tradespeople, who came largely to conquer and exploit the riches of the east, mission took on a role which was essentially a denial of the mystery of Christ's incarnation.

We need to understand the meaning of the cross not just as a weapon - in the way the Crusaders saw the form of the cross in the hilts of their swords - but rather as a lamp, a way of seeing the reality of the world: a means toward *darshana* which is a central Indian concept meaning to vision the divine present in the world. The symbol of the cross as a standing lamp is one of the great insights of the early Indian church. Light symbolism was always very important to the eastern branches of the church. We hear of the "cross of light" which appeared before Constantine. There is, however, a subtle difference between the cross understood as light and the cross seen as a lamp. The cross as light almost suggests that it was without substance and merely a spiritual ideal. But the lamp is something tangible, rooted in the ground like a tree after which it is often patterned.

There was confusion in the mind of the seafarer Vasco da Gama when he arrived on the coast of Kerala (A.M. Mundadan, "History of St Thomas' Christianity in India to the Present Day", p48. op cit "The St Thomas Christian Encyclopaedia of India.") He had assumed that he would find the kingdom of a Christian king rumoured to be in these lands and supposed to be called Prester John. John was a legendary Christian priest and ruler of a great empire originally thought to be in Asia and later associated with Ethiopia. The legend first arose in 12th century chronicles. So when the local Raja showed Vasco da Gama the temple where he worshipped he thought it was a church. The fact that it was dedicated to the Goddess Kali did not immediately confound him, though he was surprised that Mary was being depicted in this way! This confusion is somehow instructive. The fact is, that though the Christians of Kerala had been present for the previous one thousand years or more, no distinctly Christian place of worship was visible. There are various reasons we might conjecture to explain this fact. First of all, what has to be remembered is that temples were themselves in the process of evolving. Kerala was probably predominantly a Buddhist or Jain culture when Christianity first arrived. Hinduism, especially in its Brahmanical form, only became dominant after Shankara Acharya (788-820 C.E.), perhaps one of the greatest theological thinkers India has ever produced. Shankara Acharya, who lived in the ninth century, came from the Kerala area. In fact, it was the spiritual genius of Shankara, combining as he did some of the speculative insights of Buddhist thought with a new understanding of Hindu theism, that helped to eclipse the Buddhist presence in mainland India.

The form of the temple in Kerala is quite unique, having more in common with temple structures in Nepal where, surprisingly, Namboodri Brahmins from Kerala officiate in some of the major shrines, than with temple structures in neighbouring Tamilnadu. In the "History of Indian and Eastern Architecture", Percy Brown suggests influences from Kashmir while James Ferguson saw connections with the architecture of Nepal. The temple form which emerged in different parts of south India seems to derive from the "sketch temples" carved out of massive boulders on the beach of Mahaballipuram, not far from Madras. These were constructed as late as the sixth century of the Christian Era and appear to be modelled on earlier wooden forms, which are here rendered for the first time into stone.

Several writers have remarked on the influence of temple architecture on ancient Syrian churches (James Menachery ed, "The Encyclopaedia of Syrian Christianity", pp 137-149). In fact, what was more probable, was that the master crafts people who worked largely in wood, and who were consulted as to the proper location and structure of buildings, were employed by Christians and Hindus alike. They later also exerted an important influence on the way in which mosques were built in Kerala.

What is clear is that there were certain common ideas about sacred space which the Christians of Kerala shared with their

Old Syrian Church Kalupara, Kerala, showing
the skill of the Acharis in roof construction.

neighbours of other faiths. The church building was not used as a mark of identity to show how different the Christians were from everyone else. The traditional Acharis, or master craftsmen, who were not only carpenters but also local cosmologists, could relate the building to a whole spiritual world which had arisen out of the local environment. One of the striking features of the ancient churches of Kerala is how well integrated they are with the environment, not only in their use of local materials but also in the way they seem to respect natural features of the countryside such as mountains and rivers. The Acharis have a ritual science which tells them not only how the building should be suited to the land (as a bride should be suited to the bridegroom) but also how it should be proportioned. Interestingly, the Acharis were never Christian and yet it is they who often give a very characteristic form to the Syrian Christian Church building.

This does not mean that the Syrian Church has no profound understanding of the way in which the church building relates to the liturgy. In fact, perhaps more than any other Christian tradition, there is a highly developed and theological understanding of the meaning of sacred space in the Syrian tradition. This fact has not been recognised sufficiently by other branches of the church in India, which have tended to look on the Syrian Church as a very outmoded and conservative group with little sense of mission.

It is said of the mosque as it evolved in the Middle East, that what was essential was the floor space or *farsh* (Seyyed Hossein Nasr "Islamic Art and Spirituality" pp 39,45) It is here that the worshipper prostrates, facing towards Mecca. The stress in the construction of the sacred building in Kerala has been very much on the roof. In a land inundated by heavy rains, it is the roof that provides essential shelter. The skill of the Achari is in constructing the roof out of wood and bamboo. It is this roof form that gives the Kerala buildings their characteristic appearance.

Stella Kramrisch has pointed out in her monumental work on the Hindu temple (Kramrisch "Super Structure of the Hindu Temple" Journal of the Indian Society of Oriental Art, Vol XII, 1944) that the sacred place as it has evolved from folk origins in India has developed not so much from a covered space, as from an enclosed one. That is to say, going back to primordial times, it is the sacred enclosure, often defined by a grove of trees, that provided the principal *Temenos* (a sacred precinct in the form of an enclosed courtyard - Greek) out of which the later built forms emerged. Many ancient churches in Kerala, as for example at Cheriapalli in Kottayam, have an enclosing wall identical in form and function to what we find in the temple. Within this enclosure is a vertical pillar which often towers above the palm trees. This pillar, which is the tallest vertical statement, is supposed to be higher than the roof of the inner shrine. In fact, according to the manuals, or Vastu Shastras, which the Acharis follow, the roof of a building should not go higher than a palm tree, a rule which makes good sense in a land of storms and lightening flashes. The vertical focus within the sacred space of the church compound is either the tall standing cross, carved out of granite which is generally located west of the church, or the flagstaff which is surmounted by a cross and which closely resembles similar flagstaffs to be found in front of local Hindu shrines, where a flag is hoisted in honour of the deity on the principal feast day of the shrine.

These pillar or pole like forms, symbolically represent the axis, or ladder, which links heaven to earth. For Christians this has been equated with the meaning of the standing cross. This axial, cosmic symbolism of the cross is not unique to India. It is present in the Pauline doctrine of the cross as the *Stauros* (pillar - Greek) which is the tree of life. Scholars such as John Irwin of the Oriental Department of the Victoria and Albert Museum of London have pointed out the underlying symbolic link between the pillar and the cross. The Greek word *stauros* understood as cross is derived from an Indo-Aryan word meaning "that which stands firm". In the south Indian temple the connected word *sthamba* represents the "axis mundi" I would

left:
Standing cross in front of Kuruvilangad church

below:
Base of cross of Kuruvilangad

propose that the way in which the early church in India apparently understood the cross as axial, in much the same way as the high crosses of Celtic tradition drew on pre-Christian cosmic symbolism, does provide us with an important understanding of the cross in relation to other faiths. The cross is a way of re-interpreting sacred space and of connecting the Christian community with the culture of that place. So often the cross is used by the church as a way of dividing Christians from the culture of those who are not professing the faith of the gospels - a way of setting the Christian community over and against the prevailing local cultures.

In Kerala, one feels that the cross is perceived differently, as a uniting force which helps the church to become inculturated and to root itself in the most central symbols which characterise the land. The cross is the point of connection, of discovering the origins of our experience of sacred space within the cultural memory of the past. The ancient stone crosses of Kerala are what remain

Top: Winged cross at Kaduthuruthy
Centre: Granite tombstone with Syriac inscription, Kaduthuruthy
Bottom: Ancient cross with Syrian inscription, Velliapalli Church, Kottayam.

from a believing community established in pre-colonial times. It is to such a cross known as the Coonan cross that the Syrian Christians bound themselves when they decided to stand out against the colonial interests of the Portuguese who wanted them to submit to Rome.

The Portugese had used the Jesuits to impose their beliefs of the Syrian Christians The struggle became increasingly bitter and included the burning of Syrian books and documents. The dispute escalated and in 1653 at Mattanchery the stone cross of Coonan became the focus of the revolt. The majority of the Syrian Christians openly rejected the authority of the Portugese and the Jesuits by taking a public oath at the Coonan cross never to yield to Jesuit domination. In the split which followed the Syro Malabar Christians accepted the supremacy of Rome. The larger part of the Syrian Church allied themselves with the Patriarch of Antioch of the West Antioch church and became known as Jacobites.

The fact that the Coonan crosses were also used as a base

Small Gopuram over the shrine showing barrel-roof structure, Mylapore Temple, Madras

for oil lamps, in the same way that similar monolithic forms are found serving as lamp stands in Hindu and folk shrines in Kerala, also indicates how much the image of the cross was integrated into the local symbol world of Kerala. The significance of oil in Kerala, as something which gives energy and life, also pervades the ritual forms of the east. Devout worshippers bring oil as an offering to pour at the foot of the cross to fill the lamps and the oil flows so plentifully that it has to be collected in large containers after running off the plinth of the standing cross - as at Kuruvilangad, where this hallowed oil is then re-sold by the church to those who use it for healing purposes.

The Syrian Church is rich with different forms of lamps. Besides the standing lamps, which are very similar to the many varieties of lamps which we find used in traditional Hindu homes of Kerala, there are hanging lamps which have become characteristic of the Christian community. A hanging lamp is suspended in the centre of the nave and is fed with oil brought by worshippers.

One of the oldest features of the ancient church sites in Kerala is the stone cross, believed to date back to pre-colonial times. Often around these crosses can be found inscriptions in

The old Palai Cathedral

Syriac, as at the Church at Kaduthuruthy.

The cross in relation to water probably derives from the relationship of the cross to baptism in traditional Christian iconography. We have also the image of the streams of life which flow from the base of the tree of paradise. The so-called "winged cross" of Kaduthurthy is, in all probability a cross from which the river of life has its source with the branching wing-like forms, often shown in the eastern cross as emanating from the base of the cross, being representations of the gushing waters of life which well up at the foot of the cross. The cross is seen as not only the source of light but also of life, and it is in this context that it is associated with birds like the peacock and the parrot which are symbols of life and good news in Indian iconography.

Such granite crosses probably relate to the foundations of the sanctuary, which is most likely the oldest part of the church building. There are indications to show that the sanctuary was the first built structure; other buildings being added on as and when required to provide shelter for the worshippers. In that sense we can see the nave and aisles of the church as developing out of what is very similar to the *mandapam* (pillared hall) in a temple which originally was not enclosed. One of the interesting features of these ancient churches is the covered porch extending from the Church, whose intricate roof structures and carved wooden pillars are very reminiscent of local temple architecture.

The sanctuary, rectangular in plan and higher than the other parts of the church building, gives the appearance of a fortress like tower. Strangely, it is often decorated with low reliefs depicting hunting scenes. Semi-mythical creatures are found in the decoration of this sanctuary structure, which has the proportions of a double cube, the upper part of the sanctuary being, in a number of instances, made as a loft. The roof structure of this sanctuary area is internally a barrel-form with intricate carvings on the ceiling, which is panelled with wood. One might wonder if the sanctuary was originally covered by a barrel-type roof, such as we observe in some of the ancient

Left: Elephants pour water over the cross at entrance to Velliapalli Church.
Right: Typical wooden lotus carving of Syrian church.

tribal settlements not far away in the Nilgiri hills. There, for example, the Toda tribes make a sacred cow shed out of bent bamboos, creating a barrel roof. It has been suggested by some scholars that this later became the prototype for certain temple buildings: for example, the *gopuram,* which is the highly ornamented gateway of the South Indian temple. The word *gopuram* means "fortress of the cows".

The sanctuary is generally without windows, except for some quite high up, and is separated from the nave by a curtain. In some ancient Syrian Christian churches in Mesopotamia, the sanctuary veil is a series of three doors which completely shut off the holy of holies - very much as the *Garbha Griha* (holy of holies) in the temple is closed to worshippers except for the officiating priests whose function it is to mediate between the divine and the earthly.

Another basic characteristic of the Syrian Christian Church is the way in which it has evolved out of the liturgy. The very concept underlying what we call Christian liturgy seems to have had its earliest manifestation in the Aramaic world where the worship of the synagogue was adapted by the early Hebrew Christian community for the celebration of the Eucharist

Left:
The wooden pulpit
of Palai Cathedral

Above:
Detail from
base of pulpit

and other Christian rites of initiation. The cloister and enclosed house-church with its inner courtyard seems to have found its first expression in the eastern church, later to be adopted by the monastic churches of the west. It was the highly symbolic and poetic liturgies of the east which provided the original exemplars for western forms of community worship.

I like the idea of the inward-looking church - the church which evolved naturally out of the house church as found in the earliest church structure to be excavated at Dura Europos on the banks of the Euphrates. This building arises out of an ecclesiology of the hidden, often secret Church, which preserved a sense of inner mystery. The inner holy of holies and the great stone baptismal fonts remind us of the entry into the womb of the church. The baptismal font is almost buried in, and hidden away within, a recess of the thick southern wall, symbolically representing the pierced side of Christ, from whose womb-like interior the church itself, as the "New Eve" is born.

Other features familiar to local Hindu iconography are found in the decoration of the church as in the ancient cathedral of Palai where there is the form of an aquatic monster, known in Hindu iconography as the *Makara* (monster) which "acts with its mouth", symbolically swallowing and also disgorging out creation. An old wooden pulpit in the ancient Cathedral of Palai has this creature carved at the base of the pulpit. The whole pulpit structure resembles a kind of flower coming out of the gaping mouth of the monster. In the same cathedral there is also a wooden float which is carried in procession by leading members of the community and which is supposed to represent the Mountain of Paradise resting on the back of this same aquatic monster, similar to the biblical Leviat

Above the arch at the entrance of Velliapali Church in Kottayam is an image of the cross with two elephants on either side, apparently pouring water over the cross with their raised trunks. This motif is found in Hindu art, where elephants are depicted on either side of the *linga* (the sign and symbol of Shiva), or again in the image of Lakshmi (goddess of fortune) in the ritual action of pouring lustral liquids over a sacred object as a sign of worship - known in sanskrit as *Abhisheka*.

Small brass lamps which are exactly like the Hindu model can still be found but with the cross embossed on them. Similar lamps used in Hindu shrines, represent at the back the image of the goddess with elephants on either side pouring water over her. Here, instead of the image of the goddess, we find the form of the cross mounted on a firm base but without the figure of Christ on it.

A common feature in the decoration of the church, particularly in the sanctuary, is the form of the budding lotus, or the banana or plantain flower. The image of the cross emerging out of the lotus is found throughout Asia, showing the link between cross, water, and the concept of space. The lotus which has petals in multiples of eight is depicted in Indian art, from

Buddhist times, as a *mandala* (cosmic circle) from which the eight points of the compass emerge as the directions of space. At the centre of this cosmic unfolding of petals is the navel of the universe where the cosmic cross is erected as the tree or axis around which all time and space revolves.

The church, like the Hindu temple, is pictured as the body of God, whose head is in the East and whose heart, on the right side, is in the southern wall where the font is located. The veil of the sanctuary separates inner from outer, heaven from earth.

The ancient Eucharist liturgy has much in common with the Vedic *Yajna*. (sacrifice). As noted earlier, the stone Hindu temple emerged quite late, in the fifth to sixth centuries of the Christian Era. But what happened before that? How was worship conducted in Vedic times? The Vedic sacrifice was performed on a raised plinth area which formed the *Vedi*, or sacrificial altar. This was not preserved as a permanent structure. The shift towards making an actual temple took place, I would suggest, when worship patterns changed. As the Hindu idea of *Puja* (representing a series of ritual gestures intended to invoke the Presence of the deity), as distinct from the sacrificial *Yagna*, began to take prominence, the temple emerged as a permanent built form in which the deity is believed to dwell.

There has been considerable discussion among scholars on the relationship between puja and yajna. Though it is clear that puja emerged out of yajna, which is the older understanding of worship. Puja is more theistic and assumes a personal relationship of devotion between the worshipper and the revealed deity who is represented as having a visual form.

Puja is directed toward a Presence which is imagined as embodied. This Presence can also be visualised as sacred space as in the holy of holies in the Chidambaram Temple in south India where the ultimate icon is the empty space within the temple where the creator and destroyer dances as the Lord of the Dance (Nataraja).

The temple embodies this sacred space and is a place where the devotee can experience the divine Presence through the act of worship. The sense of continuing Presence which can be evoked is the essence of the temple whether in the Biblical context of Solomon's temple or in the Hindu temple. The yajna (sacrifice) invokes this Presence but does not ensure its continuance. The very nature of the yajna is that the Presence, once realised, also disappears and cannot be embodied permanently.

When the idea evolved that the divine Presence is always accessible and can be communicated the temple, and also the image it houses, became a permanent structure. This basic intuition gave expression to the earliest liturgies and is still found underlying the Syrian liturgy. The fact that the lamp is continually kept burning in the holy of holies serves to remind the faithful that the divine Presence is always there in the church.

A similar shift probably took place in biblical times when the earlier tent of meeting and moveable tabernacle, was replaced by the permanent built temple which Solomon constructed as the house of God following Babylonian patterns. The new prominence given to the king, as opposed to the earlier tribal more republican societies was, I would suggest, a deciding factor. Certainly the construction of temples in India was related closely to the rise of Hindu dynasties.

2

Colonialism and the Church

There is a need to find an Indian form of church which is not just an imitation of the kind of church which has developed in the west. For this reason there has been an effort, especially in the last fifty years, to relate the Indian church to Indian culture. Before we can understand this process it is important to clarify, as far as possible, both the terms "Indian" and "culture".

At a meeting held in Bangalore on inculturation, the theologian Teotonio Pereira who has been doing research on the relation of the church in India to the Portuguese, remarked that as far as he understood inculturation, it has arisen out of a desire in the Indian Church to free itself from the forces of colonialism. Though colonialism arose out of certain economic and political interests it did have a profound influence on culture and, in particular, the culture of Christians in the countries that had been colonised by western and so-called "Christian" nations. When the Portuguese came to India they originally came because they wanted to take control of the trade. As a newly emerging maritime power, they succeeded in putting Arab traders out of business. But in order to legitimise this venture, the Portuguese brought with them priests who were supposed to convert the natives and "save their souls".

The competition between the two Christian nations of Portugal and Spain was so great and in such danger of leading to conflict that they both appealed to Rome, as the spiritual head of the church, and asked the Pope to decide where each country should be active so that they might not interfere with each other in their efforts to explore and control the new-found worlds which lay outside Christendom. So the supreme authority of the church at that time decided where the Portuguese should have a monopoly and where Spain could take control. India fell within the influence of Portugal.

The concept of empire seems to have had a very strong impact on the whole understanding of mission. This arose from the idea of "the Holy Roman Empire" and the way in which the powerful claims of the Roman empire were later appropriated by the newly emerging states of northern Europe. The concept of Christendom mingled the political ambitions of newly converted Christian rulers with a greater dream: the belief that the earthly emperor was acting on behalf of a heavenly emperor, who was Christ himself.

The very concept of "culture", coming as it does from the word "cult", implies a kind of piety, a system of sacred symbols and practices which transcend the nation. When the Spanish conquistadors came to Asia, they brought with them not only priests but also a culture which they believed was not just something peculiar to their own local tradition but was in a way divinely ordained. That is why they assumed that the newly converted "natives" should not only adopt their beliefs but also their culture.

There is an underlying link between culture and empire. It is often said that what unites the many races which comprise the peoples of India is a common culture. Romila Thapar, Professor of Ancient Indian History at Jawaharlal Nehru University, New Delhi, suggests that originally the term *Arya* in India did not mean a race of people as that term has been understood in the west. Many races in India have come within the ambit of this all-encompassing Aryan culture. Is this culture something to do with language - for example, the Sanskrit language? India has many languages and part of the problem of the modern Indian state is that it has been understood in terms

Typical Portugese facades:
(above) Old Syrian church at Puthupally (below) Church in Cochin

of a boundary created by the prevalence of a given language and its use. But many ambiguities arise because there is a whole hierarchy of languages, some being more dominant than others, with some languages being relegated to the place of mere "dialects", whereas in fact many of India's tribal languages have an integrity and uniqueness of their own.

The concept of relating a language to a state is, according to Romila Thapar, a legacy of the European understanding of nationhood (Thapar, "The Past and Prejudice" Lecture 1, NBT, India 1972). Discussing the Indian view of the state she suggests that it evolved from an earlier understanding of lineage. The whole relationship of state to lineage is basic to an Indian approach to history. The colonialists brought not just their pattern of governance but also their own paradigm of history. That is why they misunderstood Indian culture so profoundly, viewing it as a senseless and irrational system of myths and images which seemed to them quite incoherent. Colonial culture came not only with its own ways of seeing but also, along with these assumptions, with its own peculiar brand of prejudices, or forms of blindness.

An important aspect of the colonial enterprise was to build cities. These cities were focal points of power where trade was concentrated and the resources of the land drawn in order to be transported abroad. Christianity was very much established in India as a dimension of the westernised city. This was no accident. Even in the west the church had a vital role in the "civilisation" and ultimate urbanisation of the community. The cathedral was an ecclesiastical as well as a metropolitan centre, established very much as a leading authority in the city alongside the secular authorities of the state. Here we are assuming a kind of city culture which was the inheritor of Greek and later Italian city states.

Nothing comparable really existed in Asia. Even such great temple cities like Madurai or Kanchipuram in the south, or Mathura or Varanasi in the north of India had a very different ethos from that underlying Athens or Rome, or even the more Asian cities of Ephesus or Antioch.

The Syrian Christians were a trading community, like the Jews, and it was in this capacity that their help was enlisted by the colonialists when they first reached the western coast of India. But this community was never urbanised in the way that the culture of the colonialists was. The colonial powers established cities as soon as they gained foothold on Indian soil. The cities began as fortresses and often the earliest colonial churches were within the protected bounds of these early cantonments.

The church under the colonialists became a symbol of Christian imperial power and the imposing facade of church buildings had particular significance. If we look back at the way in which the church facade developed, we might trace it to those imposing west fronts of early Romanesque, and later Gothic cathedrals, particularly in France, where the facade developed as an elaboration of the door leading into the church. These facades, as for example at Amiens in the north of France, were profound theological statements representing the last judgment and the reign of Christ over the just and also over the powers of evil. Here the facade assumed an important narrative function, being in a way a *biblia pauperum*, or bible of the poor, where they could "read" the salvation history as represented by the visible church. The west front fulfilled a similar didactic function to the elaborately decorated *gopuram* (ceremonial gateway) in the south Indian temple. By the time this feature had been taken over by the Renaissance and the Counter Reformation, its solemn role of proclaiming the symbolic way into the sacred space of the church and its catechetical function had changed. Now the facade was determined by the urban setting of the church in front of the open square or *piazza*, where it served as a kind of back-drop for the market place which generally occupied the interest of the city square. It is in this form that it was introduced into India, as a kind of ecclesiastical blessing for the secular concerns which very much characterised colonial rule. The church facade came to represent the economic and political power of the Christian community.

During the colonial period the role of the church as representative of foreign powers cannot be denied although it should not be forgotten that the church understood its rather ambiguous role in the light of a higher function which transcended national interests and was the underpinning ideology which supported a notion of empire. This concept of empire was never simply European. Asia also had dreams of empire. The modern concept of globalisation once again returns to this belief in a sense of human identity which transcends the local group, be it the clan or the nation. Great patriots like Gandhi and Rabindranath Tagore both had a deep respect for the concept of empire, although they felt that this noble ideal had been unjustly appropriated by the narrow interests of the British nation. Tagore later criticised bitterly what he suspected would become an equally narrow national interest if India were to sacrifice its belief in the universal for the sake of gaining political independence.

Colonial powers tended to patronise the church and paid for church buildings through the funds of the colonial administration. Because the church was used by colonialism for its own purposes there was an uncritical tendency amongst the majority of missionaries to accept the culture from which they had come as normative, and to impose a western culture on Indian Christians through both church buildings and forms of worship. Archbishop Menezes of Goa is a typical example of this blind acceptance of everything western as a necessary mode of being Christian. In a letter which he wrote to some important official in Rome in 1597, he expressed his desire to find a Jesuit who could be appointed as a bishop to the Syrian diocese in Kerala. He felt it would be the duty of such a prelate to...

> "purify all the churches from the heresy and errors which they hold, giving them the pure doctrines of the Catholic Faith, taking from them all the heretical books that they possess... I humbly suggest that he be instructed to extinguish little by little the Syrian language, which is not natural. His priests should learn the Latin language, because the Syrian language is a channel through which

all that is heresy flows. A good administrator ought to replace Syriac by Latin. What is most important of all is that the Bishop be a suffragan of this city (Goa) as is at present the Bishop of Cochin, his near neighbour.." (C.B. Frith, "A Short Introduction to Indian Church History, CLS).

We observe from the sentiments of this Archbishop a basic distrust of a language and form of worship with which he was unfamiliar because he was not able to understand it. In fact, one of the reasons why a local culture is suspect and an attempt is made to find some kind of universal language for the church is precisely because transparency is being sought. Local differences in idiom and culture can lead to differences in faith going unchecked.

In the Synod of Diamper, this same Archbishop Menezes systematically tried to eliminate from the ritual, as well as from the daily customs of the indigenous Christian community, all forms of assimilation of local cultural elements. The church, understood as universal, (the term "universal" here being equated with western culture), was purged of all local or distinctive features in the hope of achieving perfect unity through uniformity. This process which is in complete opposition to what we are now calling inculturation is, nevertheless, not a dead ideology. It is reappearing in the guise of globalisation: that is, the belief that in the future all cultures will become more and more alike because of scientific and technological changes and a universal culture will be discovered - which may well be the culture of a new brand of neo-colonialism.

The British, who gave a new direction to colonialism in India, built churches in important city centres in Madras, Calcutta, Bombay and, later, New Delhi which were often exact replicas of churches to be found in Britain. A favourite model was St. Martin's in the Fields, which stands at the head of Trafalgar Square in London and whose replica is found both in St Andrew's Presbyterian Church in Egmore (now Church of South India) and St Andrew's in Calcutta, near the Writer's Building, the former centre of local colonial administration.

Typical of the colonial style:
St Andrew's church in the centre of a busy Calcutta Street and
(right) St Andrew's Egmore, Madras.

It is interesting to note the appeal of a kind of classicism with Greek pillars, architraves and sometimes with domes. This classicism tended to underline the Greek and later Roman model of city planning and the church as symbol of this type of western civilisation.

This book is not a history of Church building in India, but rather a reflection on the cultural and theological significance of church construction. Other studies give a detailed picture of the way colonial churches epitomised an ideal of civilisation and culture determined by the west. These structures became an embarrassment to those Christians who had nationalist leanings. Short of actually flying the colours of a foreign rule, nothing could more explicitly represent the way in which the church was used to prop up the claims of colonialists to represent a divinely ordained empire.

Churches were conceived and built even prior to the existence of sufficient congregations to fill them. A Church Missionary Society missionary in Kerala wrote back to the Mission headquarters in London explaining that he was building churches in order to attract people to come and pray in them. (Eira Dalton "The Baker Family in India", CMS Press 1963) Consequently, the building had to be imposing with large doors and porch facing onto the street, inviting those who might enter not only to come to a faith in the gospel but also to show due allegiance to their temporal lords.

How successful this foreign model of the church became in a colonial setting remains a mystery. Despite the fact that, for example, the Syrian Christian Church in south India had been building places of worship for a thousand years before the advent of the colonial powers, and also despite its self-conscious will to survive a complete take-over by the powerful Christians of the west, the fact remains that there is hardly a single church to be found which has not been radically changed by colonial influences. The church facade is an all-pervasive feature.

As far as can be ascertained, the building of the facade from Western architectural traditions was generally paid for by the missionaries. The brick and plaster walls which were tacked on to the west end of already existing churches were welcomed as a new sign of distinctive Christian identity. As the facade in the west was related to the decoration of the apse or the sanctuary in the form of an elaborate reredos behind the high altar, this latter feature was also introduced into professed Syrian Christian churches which had no tradition of such a feature in the sanctuary.

In fact, the curtain of the sanctuary in the eastern tradition is at variance with such a decoration behind the altar. In some western churches, as we see in the rood-screens of late medieval churches in England, the earlier tradition of a separating partition between the nave and the choir or sanctuary was given this structural form. Here the screen serves a similar function to the veil, being placed in front of the altar rather than behind it, the purpose being to hide the holy of holies from the too curious.

The tendency to construct an imposing structure behind the altar is characteristic of that Latinised branch of the Syrian church known as the Syro Malabar Church. The veil of the sanctuary becomes almost like the curtain of a stage which lifts, as in a classical opera house, to reveal the grand pageantry of the ceremonial function.

There is a certain basic typology which distinguish the concept of sacred space as found in the west from that to be found in the east. The great cathedrals of the west provided a way in which the faithful could find their way from the west front, with its symbols of the struggle of light against darkness and the setting of the baptistry, towards an experience of ever-increasing light, culminating in the final revelation of the sacred mysteries in the apse in the east. Here one might find the visual equivalent of the theology of the great Pseudo Denis, called the Aeriopagite, who composed two treatises on the hierarchies both in heaven and on earth (Louis Malieckal "Yajna and Eucharist" chap IV, Dahamaram Pubns 1989). These treatises were to have a profound influence on church architecture, in that they set out a system of ascending orders whose prototype is

(top) Pillared hall (Mandapam) in front of a south Indian temple with door leading to the holy of holies (Garbha griha) or "womb house"
(below) Pillared hall (Mandapam) in north Indian palace, Panchmahal Fathepur Sikri.

Photos: courtesy of Bishop of Varanasi

to be found in the angelic spheres of heaven to which order the earthly church corresponds with its own ecclesiastical hierarchy. This framework provided the underlying theology which gave rise to Gothic forms of church building initiated by the Benedictine Monk Suger, Abbot of St. Denis in Paris. Behind this theology of hierarchical orders lies a mysticism of light and sacred numerology.

The opposite type of image related to sacred space can be found in a movement from outer visibility and light inwards to a cave-like mystery of darkness. Here the holy of holies is represented as a womb-like interior hidden from sight and only on certain occasions revealed to the discerning worshipper. Access to this inner world of mystery tends to be restricted, the worshipper being required to come to the centre through an often circuitous path. Whereas the final apotheosis of the western concept of a linear journey towards revelation is crowded with the images of redemption, the eastern tendency is to gradually empty the sacred space of all images, leaving the holy of holies dark and devoid of an excess of images in the belief that the final mystery is beyond human imagination.

Of the two approaches to sacred space which might constitute two approaches to mission itself, one an outward movement and the other more inward-oriented, colonial churches definitely favoured the former. They had a very hierarchical form of church organisation. However, in the act of imposing this kind of ecclesiology on an already existing eastern form of Christianity we find a dislocation taking place, where the built form of the church seems to be sending out different kinds of messages and there is no unity in the underlying symbol system. This underlying disunity has been a continuing problem in church building in India and we will return to it later when dealing more explicitly with the concerns of inculturation. The dislocation in the design of sacred space stems from differing perceptions of mission itself and the relation of the local to the universal.

When discussing the dynamics of culture it is important to recognise the way counter cultures operate as catalysts for

(top) Typical old village temple near Kaladi with elaborate wooden roof structure
(below) Small village temple outside Kottayam

change. A culture cannot remain static. As the Hindu temple began to assume a distinctive form of its own it also became more exclusive. Admittance to the temple, or to participation in its festivals and rites, became a means toward establishing a hierarchical order within society, demarcating the high caste from those who were to be considered impure and therefore low. The outcaste community, who represent more or less twenty percent of the Indian population, were denied temple entry.

> "The temple became yet another source of power to the Brahman. Early Hindu temples were small shrines in which the image of deity was housed. But, within a few centuries, after about A.D. 500, they developed into complex institutions built on an extensive and elaborate plan and richly endowed with the revenue of land and villages - apart from the wealth in kind collected through offerings. The management of temple funds was a source of patronage. The temples also became educational centres and provided an institutional base to brahmanical education. This facilitated the spread of ideas in an organized fashion" (Romila Thapar "The Past and Prejudice" op cit p.30).

This new role of the temple as a seat of a specialised ritual and learning also acted as a way of keeping out popular forms of spirituality, especially among those who lay outside the caste system like the Dalits and Tribals or Adivasis. The temple culture tended to become exclusivist. But the longing for access to sacred space is a universal spiritual need. It was the inclusiveness of the church, as also the mosque, which invited converts - especially from those communities who felt marginalised and rejected. We can contrast the inclusivism of an understanding of sacred space, to which all are invited whatever their social standing and lineage, with the exclusivism of a theology which denied other faith systems, along with their symbols, rejecting all forms of intercourse on the spiritual or theological plane.

Among the new converts, a sense of alienation from Hindu culture worked in the direction of separating Christian culture from all forms of local expression. The psychology of conversion included the rejection of a cultural past whose memory was hurtful and a longing for a new kind of self-image which the new faith seemed to offer. These converts did not want the church to look like the temple or anything they were familiar with, which they now actively felt the need to reject in the process of discovering a new identity. This process further reinforced a tendency to make the building for worship into a distinctly separate sign of identity.

Increasingly, Christians felt the need to make the church appear quite different from any other form of sacred building with which they were familiar. The fact that the church building offered by the missionaries was imported from distant lands added to its attraction. Further, the fact that this church building also represented power and a new form of government by which the convert felt the possibility of attaining to a new status in society was another advantage.

The Christian community, however small, now had something of which to be proud - they were assimilated into the privileges of a new ruling class and their status in society apparently changed radically.

But a new self-image is not so easily attained. Culture cannot simply be borrowed. It has to arise from the depths and be an expression of self-conscious memories. Conversion, without the process of healing these memories, cannot transform the self. That is why a theology of incarnation must insist on a process of finding one's roots in one's own cultural history.

Colonialism might have challenged the status quo but in itself it was powerless to give Christians in India a culture of their own. In fact, the cultural forms which had been taken over from those missionaries who had brought them from abroad were ultimately stifling and inhibiting to any true creativity in the Indian church. It is this basic problem that faced the Indian church at the time when nationalism became a new force striving for liberation. It is this nationalism which set the stage for efforts to find an Indian culture which is both authentic and liberating.

3

Orientalism - Shadows of the Past

In recent times many studies have examined the problem of what constitutes Indian, or even oriental, art and culture. For example: is there anything which we could call a distinctive Indian style of design?

This question has been approached from different angles. There is the social and psychological perspective which has tried to understand the ethos from which Indian forms of culture have arisen. There is the aesthetic and philosophical approach which has looked at the way in which Indian patterns of thought have influenced concepts of space and time. Then there is the more technological, craft-oriented form of analysis which has considered available materials and skills in determining local artefacts. Finally, there is the religious, or spiritual understanding, which has been concerned with the way in which aesthetics has been influenced by philosophical schools. Recently there has been much discussion concerning *Hindutva* or Hindu culture. The term Hindutva was first used by Shankara in 1917 as the title of a book. It was a seminal work for the emerging extremist Hindu party of the R.S.S. in 1926. More recently it has been revived by the politically right wing party of the B.J.P. It is literally defined as Hindu religion or culture but in practice is identified with a kind of fascism which ignores the historical reality of India and selectively glorifies aspects of tradition to foster a pan-Hindu movement to the exclusion of all else.

Hindutva has been equated in the minds of some fervent nationalists with the very essence of Indian culture. This term has even been given a race colouring, affected by the western approach to nationalism from the seventeenth century onwards, where race played an important role. Modern historians like Romila Thapar find this argument thoroughly discreditable and would argue that India is a melting pot of many races and there is no such thing as a pure race to be found in India.

In a book entitled "The making of a New Indian Art" by Tapati Guha-Thakurta (Cambridge University Press, 1992), the author has collected an impressive amount of information concerning the whole climate of opinion towards the turn of this century, especially in and around Calcutta, which led to the creation of what came to be known as the "Bengal School of Art". Guha-Thakurta shows how colonialism had produced an attitude towards Indian culture which was very derogatory but also gave rise, almost in reaction, to this negative image, to an orientalism which sometimes went to the other extreme, claiming that Indian culture was essentially spiritual, inspired by high philosophical ideals, and had an ancient history and integrity of its own. According to this view, what is distinctive about the culture of the east is its non-materialistic and idealistic nature. Guha-Thakurta, as well as Romila Thapar, are suspicious of this simplification. To characterise India as only spiritual is as misleading as to see it as only primitive, or devilish. Thapar writes :

> "The dynamics of Indian society was the juxtaposition of precept and practice, of the organisation of life as it should be, to the organisation of life as it is... The resulting dichotomies were not forced into confrontation but were adjusted. This perhaps constitutes what may be called the spirituality of India... The experience of colonialism forced India to become a participant in the industrialisation of Britain and to that extent has brought

it into the process of industrialisation in a manner specific to colonial situations. It is this which has twisted the confrontation into the false dichotomy of Indian versus western" ("The Past and Prejudice", Sardar Patel Memorial Lectures, 1972).

A new assessment of Indian culture was brought about by appreciation of its craft and design tradition. Several schools of arts and crafts were started in the major cities of India by the British. E.B. Havell was appointed principal of the Government School of Arts and Crafts in Madras and later became the head of the School of Arts and Crafts in Calcutta, There he re-organised the whole way of teaching by employing local crafts people as instructors and also insisted that students should be encouraged to study Indian works of art rather than just copy inferior models from the west. Havell played a vital role in training a whole new generation of Indian artists and was, in that capacity, a founder figure of modern Indian art. He was also an Englishman who entered into the whole debate on *Swadeshi*, which was originally a movement started by those who felt that Indian skills could be exploited by the newly developing industries where design was an important factor. The importance of Indian forms of fabric design was first recognised, at Paisley in Scotland, where a thriving industry in fabric printing made England a leading exporter of printed cloths. Other fields of design such as metal work and jewellery were also influenced. It was the argument of Havell and Coomaraswamy that architectural traditions should also be considered.

In a collection of lectures mostly delivered about 1910 in Madras, Ananda Coomaraswamy presented to the public his ideas on *Swadeshi*, a word which means "rooted in your own culture and tradition". This famous Indian art critic, who was for some time a civil servant in Sri Lanka, attacked the prejudice of those colonialists like Mr Vincent Smith who claimed that the inhabitants of Hindustan have always been "singularly indifferent to aesthetic merit, and little qualified to distinguish between good and bad art" ("On the Study of Indian Art" p.52 a lecture at the Royal Asiatic Society, London 1910 pub in"Art and Swadeshi" 1911, Reprinted by Munshiram Manoharlal, Delhi 1994).

Coomaraswamy quotes a French author to the effect that "Hindu art has been judged by most writers with injustice, for which the only excuse appears to be its extraordinary naivete, when it is not the result of a pious bigotry as exaggerated as that of the conquering Musulmans". (Op cit p.65)

In the same lecture Coomaraswamy argues passionately:

"It is perfectly useless to approach an art like Indian, armed with conventional ideas about idolatry, superstition, polytheism, priestcraft, and the like. All these things flourished exceedingly in the noblest centuries of Christian art. Every time and place has its own illusions and superstitions. The modern superstition is the superstition of facts, which is a very much more dangerous thing than any superstition of the imagination. The extremely materialistic character of most European religious thought since the Reformation has made it almost impossible for European writers to interpret the art of a people who regard a belief in the reality of phenomena as in itself the worst sort of superstition..."(Op cit p.53).

In a lecture given at the annual Ceylon Dinner in December 1911, Ananda Coomaraswamy drew the attention of his countrymen to what he calls "The Discovery of Asia":

"The far-reaching character of Asiatic influence on Europe at the present day is scarcely realised, and I think it will not be realised until we are able to look back in perspective on what has happened. Nothing of the same kind has ever taken place before. It is true, of course, that early Mediterranean civilisation was essentially of an Asiatic character. It is also true, as Professor Lethaby so eloquently tells us, that the flowering of medieval art

(above) Senate House, Madras University in the Deccani style of Moslem architecture. Photo: Dijjen
(below) Egmore Railway Station, Madras

in Europe was the result of a previous 'long filtration of the Oriental spirit to the point of saturation', but with the Renaissance the receptivity of Europe came to an end, and Asia, though in a sense more familiar, came to be regarded only as a country to be exploited" (Coomaraswamy *Education in Ceylon* in "Art and Swadeshi", p 139).

This re-appraisal of the Indian artistic heritage turned the tables on the previous rejection of eastern culture by claiming that in fact all truly spiritual art, even in the west is ultimately derived from an eastern inspiration. This "orientalism" was proposed not only by Indians in reaction to what was perceived as the negative attitude of colonialists but by enlightened Europeans like E.B. Havell, the poet Lawrence Binyon and architects like Prof. Lethaby who is quoted with approval by Coomaraswamy above. Havell argued volubly in favour of using the skills of traditional crafts people in India, especially in the construction of prominent public buildings of the Raj, that is the British rule in India from 1858 to 1947.

This tendency gave rise to new forms of colonial architecture, among which John F.Butler mentions "Madras Palladian" and "Bombay Gothic" (Butler, "Christian Art in India CLS, Madras 1986). It is in this connection that we hear of a style which is called "Indo Saracenic". This style, which became popular, can be traced back to the well-known architect William Emerson (1843-1925) who was sent to India to handle the proposed building for the Bombay School of Art in 1865. Later he became the president of the Royal Institute of British Architects and was knighted. But his heart always remained very much in India, as John Butler writes in his book on Christian Art in India (C.L.S.1986). He quotes William Emerson writing about his design for Muir College in Allahabad :

> "I determined not to follow too closely Indian art, but to avail myself of an Egyptian phase of Moslem architecture, and work it up with the Indian Saracenic style of

(above) Mokameh Shrine in Patna
Photo: courtesy of Bishop of Varanasi
(below) Old Cathedral in Agra
Photo: Paul Middleton

Beejapore and the North-West, combining the whole in a western Gothic design. The beautiful lines of the Taj Mahal influenced me in my dome over the hall, and the Indian four-centred arch suggested itself as convenient for my purpose, as working in well with the general Gothic feeling. The details show how the Gothic tracery is blended with the Indian geometrical perforated stonework in the windows, and the Caireen Moucharabyeh wood work; Gothic shafts and caps are united with Indian arches; the open staircase is also a Gothic feature adapted to Oriental requirements" (J. Mordaunt Crook "William Burges and the High Victorian Dream" Murray, London. Quoted in Butler "Christian Art in India", op cit).

John Butler comments: "Could eclecticism, and the glorying in it, go further?" This gives us some idea of the kind of mixture of styles which was taken up as a new fashion in Victorian colonial architecture. It seems also to have influenced the building of some Hindu structures, as we see in the Bellur Math of the Ramakrishna Order in Calcutta designed by a British firm of architects who later created the Mokameh shrine not far from Patna.

The tendency to use Indian architectural features as a kind of archaeological store-house of styles which could be picked up from the ruins of an exotic past, in a way, characterises a certain attitude to church architecture in the oriental mode. This approach can perhaps be traced back to the way in which the famous Agra Cathedral evolved. Begun with a grant from the emperor Akbar himself, who was inclined to collect faiths for which he had an almost kleptomaniac's fascination, the building was destroyed and then rebuilt as the fortunes of the Christians rose and fell in relation to political events and setbacks of their time.

Missionary endeavours had a chequered history, like the mission which attempted to establish itself as far north as Ladakh and then had to retreat to Nepal as it was persecuted by the Lamas. It finally ended up in Bettiah in the present dio-

Church of St Helen at Barh, Patna (Photo: Bishop of Varanasi)

Design by Fr Heras for a model church in the Indian style.
Later used as the basis for the church of St Helen at Barh, Patna.
(Based on a sketch by Heras in the Examiner newspaper)

cese of Patna, with a small remnant of Nepalese Christian families who were re-settled to form the nucleus of a Christian community in the north which dates back to the seventeenth century. It is here in Bettiah that we find another interesting attempt to create an Indian Christian architecture, which could perhaps be termed "Indo Saracenic" in so far as it seems to mingle many forms together in the hope of finding a new kind of unity (below).

It is in this context that we must attempt to understand a new tendency among some missionaries to begin using oriental features in the building of churches. Architect A. Coore, himself a member of the Cambridge Mission to India which had an important place in Delhi just at the time when Delhi was

The Bettiah Church in Patna (Photo: Bishop of Varanasi)

being made into the new capital of India, was probably influenced by the opinions of Lethaby. He wrote in an article on Indian church building:

> "...there is a strong tendency to simply reproduce all the features and arrangements to which we ourselves are accustomed and they have easily become traditional in India. The same things are seen in English churches in India, and a feeling of solidarity is produced. Now, however, another point of view has been put forward. Educated Indians have a real, if somewhat vague, desire to realise Christianity in an Indian dress, and if this is to be done, churches would not be simply copies of English ones..." (Coore. *Indian Church Building* in"Delhi No 12". Cambridge Mission to Delhi, Oct 1927).

In the same year an article written by the Jesuit Indologist Fr Heras (The Examiner, Oct 22, 1927) spoke of his dream of a church to be constructed in the manner of a South Indian temple. In November 1953 the magazine "Liturgical Arts" published an illustration of a proposed church in Barh in the diocese of Patna which was an attempt realise the dream of Fr Heras. The fact that Heras was thinking of using the south Indian Dravidian temple as a model for church design shows how much of a pioneer he was in the field of architectural adaption though it took another 30 years before his ideas became a reality.

In Madras in 1921 a Quaker architect by the name of Reginald Dann was appointed director of town planning. There was a small but active group of the Society of Friends in Madras at the time among whom were Frederic Gravely, superintendent of the Madras Government Museum and Edward Barnes who was teaching science at the Madras Christian College. Later, Marjorie Sykes was also to join the group on the staff of the Bentinck Girls High School, where she became the principal before leaving to join the freedom struggle along with Gandhi and Rabindranath Tagore.

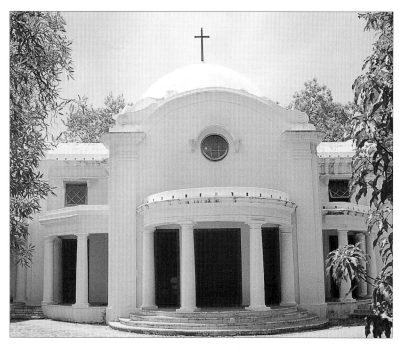

The entrance and the interior of the chapel at the
Women's Christian College, Madras, built 1923

Reginald Dann was invited to design the new chapel for the Women's Christian College in Madras, which had been founded in 1915. This chapel was completed in 1923, and Dann wrote of it :

"We have attempted, with freedom and imagination, without slavish imitation of any particular building or style, to be obedient to the lessons of perfection in proportion and style handed down from the past, so far as they are applicable to present needs" (C. Hargreaves "Twenty-five Indian Churches", p.25, ISPCK 1975).

Cecil Hargreaves, in his booklet on twenty-five Indian churches, adds that Dann's aim had been "to build mostly in simple style, using simple materials: common country brick arches, whitewashed walls and dome, and Cuddapah stone floor." Marjorie Sykes, in her book on Indian Quakers, writes of Reginald Dann that he had a great appreciation of Indian architecture, of which he said: "infinite patience and indomitable courage have gone into these monuments of man's creative capacity... developed through centuries to meet the challenge of climate and availability of material" (Majorie Sykes, "An Indian Tapestry: Quaker Threads in the History of India, Pakistan and Bangladesh", p.206,7, Sessions Book Trust, England 1997). He stressed that the modern architect ought to study these things with humility so that his own work may be "humanized and indianized". I feel that there is much in common between the chapel of the Madras Women's Christian College, designed by Reginald Dann, and Alfred Coore's building at Turkman Gate (see next page) which, incidentally, would have been at the heart of colonial India if it had not been for a riot at Turkman Gate which led to the British Government deciding to shift the new capital to its present site known as New Delhi.

The discussion over styles was often reduced to a preference for particular forms of decoration, what E.B. Havell scornfully referred to as....

"tricking out the business arrangements of the Anglo-Indian administration in tinsel adornments called "styles". The official architect sits in his office at Simla, Calcutta, or Bombay, surrounded by pattern books of styles - Renaissance, Gothic, Indo-Saracenic, and the like - and having calculated precisely the dimensions and arrangement of a building suited to departmental requirements, offers for approval a choice of the "styles" which please him or his superiors, for clothing the structure with architectural garments in varying degrees of smartness, according to the purpose for which it is intended, at so much per square foot" (Indian Architecture, Its Psychology, Structure and History from Muhammadan Invasion to the Present Day"pp 221-223, pub London 1913).

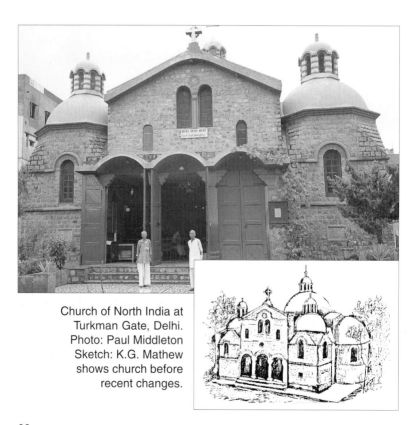

Church of North India at Turkman Gate, Delhi.
Photo: Paul Middleton
Sketch: K.G. Mathew shows church before recent changes.

As Havell repeatedly stated, when he was advocating a return to Indian traditions of building, his concern was not simply with superficial decoration. He had shown the great riches of an Indian craft tradition which he claimed was comparable to the craft tradition of medieval Europe, when the builder was also the architect. We observed this was the case in Kerala, where the Achari simultaneously designs and builds. The problem with colonial architecture was that the designers were imported from Europe and were divorced from the actual local builders. This meant that, except for a few like Reginald Dann, the foreign architect was unfamiliar with local building traditions, materials, and environmental conditions, imposing on a subject people a style of building suited to the west. The local skilled crafts person only became a tool, whose creative powers were never acknowledged or drawn upon.

Ananda Coomaraswamy in 1908 pointed to the cause of the decline of creative arts in India and Ceylon as originating in this basic distrust of the creative capacities of the natives.

"the cause of the decline of the arts has been the growth of commercialism - that system of production under which the work of European machines and machine-like men has driven the village weaver from his loom, the craftsman from his tools, the ploughman from his songs, and has divorced art from labour" (Coomaraswamy, "The Medieval Sinhalese Art", p 53)

The problem is therefore identified as arising from a whole system of exploitation and not merely from a rejection of the local culture. Whereas the Muslims had often destroyed temples and had their own clear ideas of what sacred buildings should be, they always channelled local talent and allowed the crafts of India to flourish. This is why there is a rich tradition of Islamic architecture in India. But the Christian colonialists, in particular the British, while insisting on a European model of education, totally disregarded the local systems of knowledge which were dismissed as unscientific and irrelevant.

Largely this was because it was seen that indigenous patterns of thought were deeply imbued with an intuitive, symbolic and mythical way of perceiving reality and this was anathema to those who felt that rational western patterns of thought were normative.

This attitude of deep repugnance for the very ethos from which Indian culture derives its energy is shared by some of the great architects of modern India. Architects are trained, in the same way that art students are trained in the visual arts by using western ways of understanding. The modern architect Le Corbusier was as scornful of Indian cultural tradition as the earlier colonial E.L. Lutyens had been when designing New Delhi. When asked why he had not spent much time studying Indian traditions of architecture, Le Corbusier jokingly said it was because he was afraid of being bitten by a snake. Undoubtedly Freud would have seen some significance in this remark! The snake was probably for him a symbol of the whole of Indian culture. The modern architect, particularly a city planner, believes it is only those rational, scientific patterns of thought that characterise modern western culture which are most appropriate.

This tendency to reject other ways of thinking has nothing particularly to do with the gospel but it has much to do with such missionaries as Alexander Duff, who believed that the task of the church was to bring to the irrational, superstitious cultures of the east the light of reason which would ultimately lead to the light of Christ. Nehru, who was critical of the grandiose style of Lutyens, saw New Delhi as a symbol of the pretensions of Britain as the creators of an empire but he was equally critical of Indian traditional buildings. In a talk which he gave at the inauguration of a national seminar on architecture in 1959 he was very candid about his feelings. He said:

> "Mr Humayun Kabir referred to the great temples of the south and the Taj Mahal. Well, they are beautiful. Some of the temples of the south, however, repel me in spite of their beauty. I just can't stand them. Why ? I do not know.

I cannot explain that, but they are oppressive, they suppress my spirit. They do not allow me to rise, they keep me down. The dark corridors - I like the sun and air, and not dark corridors. All architecture represents to a large extent the age in which it grows. You cannot isolate architecture from the age, from the social conditions, from the thinking, the objectives, and ideas of that particular age. Mr Kabir refers to the static condition in regard to architecture in India during the last two or three hundred years. That really was a reflection of the static condition of the Indian mind, and Indian conditions. Everything was static. In fact India was static before that...." (The Madras Group "By Traditions Unfettered - a study of Modern Architecture in the Third World Context" p.66).

These are the views of the man who led India into the modern world and wrote eloquently about the discovery of India. We can see how much his mind had been conditioned by a certain type of western education. When looking at the way in which English architects like Alfred Coore and Reginald Dann drew elements of which they approved from Indian culture, one can see the same stress on a kind of rational order, which could accept the decorative but keep clear of any deeper encounter with the *Mysterium Tremendum* of which the temple is an expression. For them the great icons of the temple were equally impossible to appreciate.

Visiting the chapel which Reginald Dann designed for Bentinck Girls School (top of next page) one is struck by its emptiness.

For John Butler (who was also very suspicious of Hindu symbolism) this chapel is "an outstandingly successful example of adapting a temple *mandapam* or open hall type of a village shrine" ("Twenty-Five Indian Churches" op cit). This chapel was built in 1932, almost a decade after the earlier chapel which Dann designed for the Madras Christian Women's College. Here, we are told, the new interest which Marjorie Sykes had found in the freedom struggle and the ashram model of Tagore

69

at Shantiniketan found expression. But perhaps their Quaker leanings made it an expression singularly devoid of any imagery. Governor General, Lord Bentinck, after whom this institution was named, "considered Indian art so lightly that he was only diverted from selling the Taj Mahal for the value of its marble because the proceeds of a test auction of materials from the Agra Palace proved unsatisfactory". (E.B. Havell, "Indian Sculpture and Painting", p.246, London 1928) Those who have shown interest in India's development, particularly the education of its masses, have not necessarily been sensitive to its artistic heritage. Gandhi himself, for all his support of Swadeshi crafts and khadi, evinced little passion for the arts.

Alfred Coore, writing about his work in designing the church in Mehrauli, built in 1928 said:

> "The new Church which is being built in Mehrauli follows entirely the Indian conception of a house looking inwards. It is an attempt to supply a building suited not only to Indian conditions, but also to the special circumstances of the Mehrauli Congregation.
> The Church stands on rising ground under the shadow of the Qutb Minar, where an old Mohammedan Mosque was built from the fragments of Hindu temples. That has

now fallen into decay, and is an interesting ruin ; but the Church, though small and humble is being built up" ("Delhi", Oct 27 op cit p 232).

The image is persuasive. The church is being built on the ruins of preceding civilisations which are interesting and perhaps can be adapted for present use. The Mehrauli Church uses, in quite an imaginative way, an old ruined fort of the earlier Delhi Sultanate. It has been converted into the shell for a church with a Hindu type *sikhara* or crown rising from within the cloistered courtyard. Here we find a kind of synthesis which has been given to the local church by missionaries who come from outside (see below and next page).

The Almut Memorial Church in Mehrauli built by A, Coore. (photo: Paul Middleton)

Sketch below shows whole complex.

Coore wrote of this church:

> "The older members of the Mission, Lefroy, Allnut and Carlyon, used to hold almost as an axiom, and we all agreed, that we must provide new-born congregations with churches. We gave them the Gospel, taught them to worship a congregation must worship somewhere. They needed a building, they were mostly very poor, so we gave them a place to worship in." (Alfred Coore, "Delhi", Indian Church Building, Oct 27 op cit p.205)

This gift of a church is also characterised by such buildings as the church at Lashkar, (next page) patronised by the Italian adventurer John Baptist Filose whose son Michael helped to design the palace of the Scindias using the skills of local craftsmen. These craftsmen of Gwalior and Lashkar were the inheritors of a long tradition of fine building going back to the palace on the Fort of Gwalior, from which even the Moghuls had earlier drawn elements to create their own distinctive style of architecture in north India.

But the relationship of the missionary to the local church and its surrounding culture as a basis for understanding how a new attitude towards indigenous traditions began to replace the kind of rejection of other religions which characterised both Portugese and British colonial rule. For the colonialists, their Christianity came to represent their superiority. Even when they did not openly claim to evangelise in the way earlier Portuguese colonialists had attempted to by bringing along with them their soldiers and their *padres,* or priests, the British who introduced the concept of the secular state and parliamentary democracy, tried to stamp out what they perceived as pagan superstitions. This attitude of cultural superiority is still to be found within churches in India today.

Church of John the Baptist, Lashkar, Gwalior (Photo: Bishop of Varanasi)

4

The Missionary and the Local Church

The traditional missionary could be described as a vertical invader, coming to evangelise a land not only from far away geographically, but also from another plane of reality - a different perception of history. The missionary intervenes from above, being inserted into a culture from another level. It is in this sense that a missionary has been understood as different from a tourist or a pilgrim.

The missionary, at least in the early days of colonialism when the Portuguese first came to India, felt able to accompany those who came to colonise. When the Dutch and British came to India, the relationship between missionary and colonialist became strained. There was a perceived difference between the role which the missionary assumed as a saver of souls and the commercial interests of the colonial authorities. The sensitive and committed among the missionaries recognised that their task was to come in between the rampant self interest of colonial agents and the colonised in some way - at least to protect those who had now joined the church. The colonial powers were suspicious of the undertakings of missionaries, fearing they would not always be loyal agents of the country from which they had originally come.

On the other hand, the missionary did not feel committed to local nationalist hopes. Often, the missionary fully supported the concept of empire and even lent it a moral authority which was understood as legitimising foreign rule. This meant that when Indians began to struggle for self rule and a new nationalism began to take shape, missionaries were seldom sympathetic and, to some extent, even opposed such aspirations. Most missionaries were fiercely critical of nationalist leaders like Gandhi whom they perceived as a threat. Where they recognised the moral authority with which he spoke they attempted to appropriate his initiatives, claiming that he was using a prophetic language which he had borrowed from the biblical tradition. Missionaries tried to insist that what gave Gandhi's stand moral force was a kind of Christian message. It upset them that he refused to become a Christian. He said that though he respected the Jesus of history, whom he called a true *satyagrahi*, one committed to a political stand for the sake of truth, he considered the visible church which he saw in India as a betrayal of the gospel message. Many Hindu leaders in recent times have said that though they believe in the message of Christ which is found in the gospels, they do not believe in the institutional church.

Gandhi insisted that his moral position owed much to the *Bhagavad Gita*, the Hindu scripture to which he felt most committed and which he tried to re-interpret in the light of modern political events. He also pointed to the concept of *dharma* (righteousness) and *ahimsa* (non-violence) to be found in the Jain and Buddhist traditions of India, as providing a spiritual source from which he had drawn inspiration.

The witness of men like Gandhi, Rabindranath Tagore, Vivekananda, Raja Ram Mohan Roy and other leading thinkers of what might be called the reformed Hindu tradition of the late nineteenth and early twentieth century in India, had a deep impact on certain thinking Christians. It raised a new awareness among them that they needed to find an Indian approach to theology. From the *Brahmo* movement initiated by Raja Ram Mohan Roy and Divendranath Tagore, father of the poet Rabindranath Tagore, a new perception of what P. C. Mazoomdar called the "Oriental Christ" arose. Reformed Hindus were able to claim that Christ was a guru, very similar in many ways to Hindu gurus and that he was an Asian and closer to the Asian tradition of spirituality than the religious attitudes of the west which owe so much to the rather legalistic attitudes of Rome.

Sri Ramakrishna had a vision of Christ as he sat in meditation on the banks of the Hooghly at Kalighat. He felt that this Jesus whom he worshipped, had stepped inside his own body and had become a part of his innermost consciousness. Later, the Ramakrishna order was founded on Christmas day 1897 by Swami Vivekananda. There are a number of aspects characteristic of this order which appear to derive from the organisational structures to be found in the church. Even the pattern of worship to be found among the Brahmos and also such reformed sects of Hinduism as the Ramakrishna order and later, the Aurobindo Ashram and the followers of Ramana Maharshi, indicate how Hinduism was influenced by the congregational worship which characterised Christian liturgy. There is an interplay between temple architecture among these reformed Hindu movements and a newly-emerging Indian Christian church building. As noted earlier, the shrine at Mokameh in Patna diocese is very similar to the Belur Math of the Ramakrishna order. In Bangalore a temple of Ramana Maharshi was recently constructed which looks very much like a church.

Keshab Chander Sen, a leading figure of the Brahmo movement, laid the foundations for what is now termed an "Indian Christian theology". This was further developed by Brahmabandhab Upadhyay, who called himself a "Hindu Christian". He was never really accepted in his life by any official church. Although he was baptised into the Roman Catholic Church, he was later repudiated by the authorities of this church for mixing Hindu concepts with his Christian faith, and also for his politicised nationalist leanings. Brahmabandhab Upadhyay has more recently been compared by Bishop Lakshman Wickremesinghe to Clement of Alexandria, a Father of the Church, who attempted to find a new synthesis between the essentially Semitic mindset of Jesus and his first disciples, and the philosophical traditions of the Greco-Roman world. What Clement of Alexandria did in giving a basis to Christian theological reflection in the philosophical schools of the Greeks, Brahmabandhab attempted to do by outlining what he considered to be a Christian Vedanta.

The nationalist movement in India did act as a catalyst for the kind of faith reflection which has come to be known as inculturation Even outside the area of religious thought, there has been much discussion in recent times about the relationship of culture to national identity. "Style", like the term "decoration", is thought of as something superficial, an external coating so to speak, which give a particular appearance to an essential kernel that is thought to be universal. Sadhu Sundar Singh spoke of wanting to have the "waters of eternal life in an Indian vessel". What the Indianisers were attempting went further than the efforts of the "orientalists". The Indianisers spoke of Christianity being baptised in the waters of Indian spirituality. They introduced a new image: the gospel itself needed to enter into the waters of the Ganges to emerge as something not just foreign but truly part of Indian culture. When, for example, Keshab Chander Sen and, later, Brahmabandhab Upadhyay related the Hindu concept of *Sat Chit Ananda* (Truth, Consciousness, Joy) to the Christian understanding of Trinity, they were touching at the very heart of theological discourse. What was the meaning of the person of God? In what way can we comprehend the incarnation of God into a human person ? What is the meaning of the Spirit, and the way in which the Spirit speaks to the heart, inspiring the innermost core of the human being? Can we equate the *Pneuma* of the Greeks with the *Atman* of Hindu speculative thought? In what sense can we say that God is beyond both name and form? These questions, though very much a part of the highly theoretical and discursive thought of speculative thinkers both in the east anmd the west, did affect the way in which the Holy Place was understood: as a manifestation to the human senses of the eternal within time and space.

An example of this process of Indianising the church would be the way in which Christians who were deeply impressed by Indian forms of spirituality began to look at the meaning of the womb-house (*Garbha griha*) of the Hindu temple-shrine, as related to the ancient concept of the *Guha*, or "cave of the heart". Could this very vital image, to be found in the architecture of the Hindu temple, be absorbed into a Christian understanding of the presence of God within the body of the church? As the construction of modern Hindu prayer rooms, or places for religious assemblies, had been affected by the forms evolved in church architecture for congregational worship, now the form of the church in India was being changed by the Hindu concept of an inner sanctum sanctorum, which is like the womb of sacred space. Linked with this intuition was the image of God as a mother and not simply the father figure which had come to be the dominant mode of picturing God in Judeo-Christian tradition.

The adaptation of this idea of the womb into the structure of the Indian church led to the incorporation into an Indianised form of liturgy of such ritual gestures as *Arathi*. The image which we have of the divine does affect the way in which we conceive of that divinity incarnated into the world and as we perceive it with our senses. The temple represents the body of God. God is incarnated not only in the person of the historical Jesus but through the built forms where the divine presence continues to inspire devotion, leading individual worshippers to an experience of the continuing intervention of the divine within human cultures. It is this belief in the incarnation which has inspired those Indianisers who have depicted Jesus as an Indian, and not just as the historical person who was a Jew. This Jesus is experienced by the worshipper as continually being born into the reality of the world today, in and through the lives of those who are perceived as being made in his image.

The first artists in India to try and depict Jesus as an Indian, like Jamini Roy in Bengal and K.C.S. Panikkar in Madras, have stressed the message of liberation from an oppressive foreign rule which they felt underlay the life and gospel of Jesus. The modern Indian painter Kishen Khanna has repeatedly represented Jesus in his paintings but the Jesus he depicts is not the conventional Jesus one might find in a Portuguese church in Goa who is generally portrayed looking very much like the Portuguese authorities who came to rule over Goa. The Indian Jesus is like a folk hero, having the appearance of those whom he came to liberate. Kishen Khanna has clearly identified Jesus with the struggles of the suffering masses. When I asked Kishen Khanna why the image of Jesus had appealed to him, he explained that for him Jesus represents the predicament of many Indians today who find themselves torn between colonial powers on the one hand and a narrow religious nationalism on the other hand.

The historical Jesus also faced this kind of cultural dichotomy; there was the power of the Roman empire but also a Jewish nationalism which had a tendency to manifest itself in forms of religious bigotry. When a community equates religious beliefs with national identity there is great danger of confusing spiritual realities with political opportunism. An artist or poet, such as Rabindranath Tagore, feels called on to assert the freedom of the individual beyond such narrow exigencies, by pointing to a universal humanism transcending race and creed. In a strange way, by depicting the Jesus of history as an ordinary Indian, they attempt to show him as a universal figure who could not be appropriated by colonial powers, and made to serve their vested interests. This figure of the oriental Christ counteracts the Jesus image which has tended to depict him as a foreign ruler. The image of Jesus, like the built form of the Christian place of worship does represent an understanding of his power as on the side of the rulers or on the side of those who are oppressed.

Alongside the problem of nationalism is the question of pluralism. The missionaries who came to India generally held their particular religious forms of worship as being absolute and normative for everyone.

Father Bede Griffiths once told me that he did not consider himself to be a missionary but rather a pilgrim. True, he had come from a distant land to discover India and to search for

God in India. He came motivated by a deep personal faith in Jesus and commitment to the gospels. He also came to India not only to give or share his experience of faith but also to deepen his own experience of the spiritual world through a living encounter with another religious tradition. This meant that when he came to India he came as it were to a "holy land" to worship in the holy places that he found in India. His attitude towards the temples which he visited could be paralleled by the way in which Fr. Jules Monchanin came to India a few years earlier. In an essay written soon after Fr. Monchanin's death in 1957, there was the following account of how he tried to create within his ashram of Shantivanam a small chapel which encapsulated all that he admired within the Hindu Temple.

"He never entered a temple without respect: for centuries people had gathered there in search of the 'presence', the sannidhi; how could God have refused Himself to such a sincere and ardent devotion? When in Pondicherry he followed with special interest the restoration of a small but beautiful "Chola" shrine of Magadipettu and his dream was that the sanctuary of his ashram should be a reproduction of Magadipettu...
"In 1951 a modest oratory was built under the shade of the ashram; the small square room of the mulasthanam (sanctuary), dark and bare save for an altar and tabernacle of roughly hewn granite and a few brass oil lamps. Despite the very limited means available, something had been recaptured in its simplicity and nakedness, of the holy, the mysterious, the 'numinous' which characterises the sanctuary of the Hindu temple - yet at the same time it was no slavish copy."
(Swami Parama Arubi Anandam: "Glimpses of the Life and Ideals of Fr. J Monchanin, 1895-1957", Saccidananda Ashram, 1959. pp.46-47.)

Fr Monchanin actually only constructed the Garbha griha

and it was Fr Bede Griffiths who later completed the building according to Fr Monchanin's plans by adding the Vimana (carved dome) executed by local village craftsmen (opposite page).

One way of understanding the evolution of the Hindu temple is to understand the way in which a popular passion for pilgrimage was encouraged, starting with the emperor Asoka who felt that by supporting pilgrimage centres all over his empire his people would have a greater sense of belonging and different races and cultures would come together. Later the great Hindu reformer and thinker, the Adi Shankaracharya, established pilgrimage centres all over India, from the southern tip of the Indian peninsular to its northern reaches in the Himalayas.

The idea of pilgrimage has influenced the very structure of the Hindu temple in the same way that important pilgrimage centres of Europe affected the architecture of cathedrals which became the focus for pilgrims moving right across Europe, either on their way to Compostella in the South or, as in England, journeying to Canterbury. Whereas the Church is primarily conceived of as a place where a community gather to sit or stand still to listen to the Word of God, pilgrimage pre-supposes a moving community who are travelling from one shrine to another. This means that a pilgrimage centre has to accommodate a travelling community, not only in terms of providing lodging for pilgrims but also giving them a chance to pay their respects to different holy places within the overall plan of the sacred site. The pilgrimage centre thus develops into a complex of buildings which serve the different needs of the shifting community.

The image of Jesus the pilgrim leads to a theology of welcoming and also an image of the holy place as offering hospitality. Such a theology changes our understanding of mission and an ecclesiology giving rise to the idea of a pilgrim church. However, there are tensions involved, as we see from an account given by Bishop Lakshman Wickremesinghe of Sri Lanka concerning a visit he paid to an important pilgrimage centre in his own country in the company of the Archbishop of Canter-

Shantivanam Ashram

(above) the Vimanam showing Christ and Mary

(right) Ashram chapel and library
(photo: Caroline MacKenzie)

bury. Bishop Lakshman Wickremesinghe was, until his tragic death whilst trying to visit Tamil refugee camps after the eruption of ethnic violence in his land in 1983, a leading personality in his country who had thought deeply about the importance of religious dialogue with neighbouring Buddhist monastic communities. He discusses his own understanding of inculturation in an essay entitled "Christianity moving Eastwards"

> "Architecture, sculpture and painting, music, lyrics, dance and drama, incense, lights and flowers are used within the diocese, especially when we keep festivals of one kind or another. Historical narratives, folk tales, and scriptural stories from the Sinhala-Buddhist tradition have been used for preaching and religious instruction" (Wickremesinghe article *Christianity moving Eastwards,* "CTC Bulletin" 1995 p.61, pub CCA,HK).

He then recounts how he accompanied the Archbishop of Canterbury to visit the Temple of the Tooth, which is the most important shrine of Sinhalese Buddhism. This shrine houses a very precious relic of the Lord Buddha and can be compared with Canterbury Cathedral which was also a focus for pilgrimage in the Middle Ages because it housed the relics of St. Thomas of Canterbury.

> "We made certain gestures. We removed our footwear as is the custom. For us it was an act of reverence to Gautama the Buddha as a religious leader of spiritual insight and moral stature, whose relic was a continuing symbol of his historic personality and acknowledged saintliness.... We also permitted the monks to chant blessings upon us, which they wished to do out of respect and goodwill to an international religious leader. However, we did not place our folded hands in front of our breasts with bowed heads as the Buddhists among us did, because we did not accept the interpretation of this

blessing in the texts they chanted" (Wickremesinghe op cit p.62).

One might compare the way in which these visitors responded to the welcome offered with the passage in the gospel where we are told that Jesus sent out his disciples on the first mission, asking them to carry nothing with them except the very bare minimum and to seek hospitality from the homes of those they went to, bringing only a blessing with them on those who might offer a welcome. The sacred place is regarded as the home of God and much of the ritual associated with the temple is related to the act of recognising the presence of the Lord within the temple. But the temple is not only a home for the deity, it is also the spiritual home of the whole community. In the past, Christian missionaries have on occasion destroyed a local temple and then built a church on its ruins in recognition of the fact that the place still remains holy for the community. Even in Goa, a number of churches were built on the very sites where temples formerly stood. Bom Jesu in Old Goa, for example, has beneath it the ruins of an earlier Hindu temple. This policy of using sacred sites which had been for centuries the focus of the religious feeling of the community was practiced right across Europe. Many of the great pilgrimage centres and cathedrals are built upon holy land which earlier, before the arrival of Christian missionaries, provided a spiritual home for the people.

A number of churches in India have responded to the important place of pilgrimage in Indian culture. The little chapel built on a hill in the borderland country between Tamilnadu and Andhra Pradesh is an example of a very effective re-interpretation of a wayside pilgrimage centre (next page).

When I visited this simple open-air structure overlooking a wide panoramic view of the ghats, I was very much struck to find there a young man sitting alone reading the Bible. It was the season of Lent and the young man said that he had come there to fast and to wait for a call from God. He felt that this was a turning point in his life and that he was meant to leave

his work in the world to become a wandering preacher. Perhaps he will in the future be cast in the mould of a kind of evangelical minister who goes from village to village announcing the gospel. Perhaps he was not even conscious of the way in which he was also living out a cultural pattern which extended beyond Christianity and had much in common with the kind of calling which Sanyassis like Ramana Maharshi felt when he left home as a young man to go and live in silence on the holy mountain of Tiruvanamalai in Tamilnadu, not too far away from Zion Hill. There is an intuitive cultural patterning which is not often consciously realised. Ultimately, it is these deep underlying currents of life which give a sense of indigenous context to a particular community. They have little to do with the way in which creeds are articulated and theologies are constructed to explain a reality which has its source in life and inner spiritual experience. Pilgrimages are related to festival seasons which reflect the rhythms of the Indian climate. The church, if it is to be a part of the Indian landscape, must celebrate the way in which nature itself is felt to be holy in India.

The relation of guest to host is a very complex one and the metaphor can be followed through into the very structure of the liturgy. The missionary is a guest and the local culture and church represent the host but there is a tension between the foreign missionary and rising political nationalism. The missionary appears as an intrusive agent who can undermine local identities. It has often been very difficult for a missionary who has a very powerful position in decision-making, to change the role of being a "parent" and to accept a different position as a friend or even servant.

New missionary orders or groups which have emerged in recent times have tried to establish a new pattern of relationships with local churches and the wider community. An example of this would be the Society of the Auxiliaries of the Missions (SAM), inspired by the ideals of Vincent Lebbe, a missionary to China. Both Fr. Jules Monchanin, founder of Shantivanam Ashram and Fr. James Tombeur belonged to this group. In the touching account of his ministry as a priest in the Kotar Diocese in South India, Fr. James Tombeur writes of the inspiration of Vincent Lebbe who "was Chinese in all that he was and did, one with the aspirations of his people" (James Tombeur "Led by God's Hand" p.152 pub Nalini Nayak, Trivandrum 1990). He writes of the role which Vincent Lebbe played in his own life, inspiring him to build "churches which would not remind the people of the foreign character of their religion, integrating Indian culture, symbols, customs and traditions in people's worship". Fr James Tombeur, in his account of how he came to build a group of village churches where he was very active in organising the people, often insists that he took the whole community into his confidence and asked them to suggest ways in which they would like their parish church to be built. When designing one church, he suggested that the parish council should go on a kind of pilgrimage to visit the great Hindu temple at Madhurai. After this trip, they decided that they would like to have a *gopuram* at the entrance of their church which was constructed very much on the lines of a village temple shrine. The local palace of the Hindu kings at Padmanabhapuram was a source of inspiration for another village church. The parishioners of Fr James' churches were simple toddy tappers or fishermen for whom becoming Christian was also a way of aspiring to a new status in society. To construct a church in the form of a temple was probably a way for them to assert that they were not to be considered as outside the Hindu tradition, in which they had formerly been rejected communities, relegated to a position outside the caste system.

Church at Melpalai built by James Tombeur

The Nallayanpuram church - Photo James Tombeur

Finally, with failing health, James Tombeur decided to establish his own ashram community, which he called an open ashram of contemplation at the service of the poor ("Led by God's Hand", op cit 1990). This ideal of an ashram both contemplative and at the service of the local community has also been the inspiration of others like the Little Brothers and Sisters of Jesus, following the spiritual journey of Brother Charles de Foucauld. They have a common spirituality which tries to discover the hidden life of Jesus in Nazareth. The small communities living in this spirit seek to identify themselves with ordinary villagers or slum-dwellers, avoiding as far as possible positions of power or influence in society. They live among the people, choosing the kind of house which is the typical home in the neighbourhood, seeking to make it into a "Nazareth".

Another group, though very small in numbers and marginal when thinking of the general ethos of the Christian communities in India, is the Society of Friends known as Quakers. Marjorie Sykes gives some telling insights into the lives of individual Quakers who came to India and often identified with important freedom fighters like Gandhi. She quotes Pandit Govind Ram who said to Charles Gayford, a young English Quaker in 1875 that "life should be lived as Jesus taught. But don't create a separate Christian caste. Let the spirit of Christ transform Indian society from within" (Majorie Sykes "Indian Tapestry" p.71 Pub: Sessions Book Trust 1997). It is this effort to model the local Church on the life of Jesus of Nazareth that constitutes a new understanding of mission in India.

5

The Ashram and Architecture

Ashrams have made a disproportionately large contribution to the indianisation of Church architecture. Three out of the 25 Churches recently written up, are actually ashram chapels. (Cecil Hargreaves, 25 Indian Churches, Delhi ISPCK 1975.) Important Indian liturgical contributions have come from Poona, Shantivanam, Jyotiniketan and a few other ashrams. And the contributions to Indian Christian lyrics have come at least from Tirupattur and from N.V. Tilak who founded an early ashram."(Richard Taylor "Christian Ashrams as a Style of Mission in India", IRM, July 1979)

Among significant ashrams is Gyan Ashram which was founded soon after the Eucharistic congress in Bombay in the early sixties. Fr George Proksh of the S.V.D. order, started a *sangeetayan* or school for Indian dance, music and singing where "he introduced young Christians to the richness of Indian culture and inspired them to bring the good news to all their brethren in India in a way they could appreciate and understand. It was especially through the great dance drama like Meshpal Bhagvani (Shepherd God) that he enthused thousands all over India and on his many tours in Europe. In the tradition of the great dance-dramas like Ramlila, or Krishnalila, this "Christlila" was a unique and harmonious blend of the different classical dances and various folkdances." (Hargenmayer, "A History of Gyan Ashram of Guru Gyan Prakash" 1985) This ashram is now headed by the well-known dancer priest Francis Barbosa. Also emanating from this ashram are many popular *bhajans* which are used as devotional songs in churches all over India.

It was in the spirit of Gyan Ashram that an art ashram was founded in 1983 with the encouragement of Fr. Matthew Lederle who was then secretary of the Ashram Aikya, a fellowship of Christian ashrams. He had started *Snehasadan* in a Hindu part of Pune city, to serve as a centre for dialogue between people of different faiths and also as a place for the study of Indian cultures. Art India, a publishing concern, was established to encourage Indian artists by printing their works on Christian themes.

A number of Christian thinkers have discussed the history of modern Indian Christian ashrams which were inspired by the renaissance of ashrams which was an important aspect of the Hindu reform movement towards the end of the last century. Though ashrams existed in Indian society from very ancient times, they were given a new significance by neo-Hindu movements like the *Brahmo Samaj*. It was felt the ashram could provide an inspiration for the renewal of Indian society by offering a model of selfless service to the community and a willingness to sacrifice all personal ambition in order that the whole society might find a new sense of purpose. According to Richard Taylor, the earliest modern ashram following this pattern was *Bharat*, founded in 1872 at Belgharia near Calcutta by Keshub Chander Sen who had strong Christian leanings. This was soon followed by *Santiniketan*, founded by Debendranath Tagore, father of the poet Rabindranath, in 1888. Rabindranath Tagore decided to settle down in this ashram in 1901 and later founded his famous school there, which gradually developed into his vision of *Viswa Bharati*, an Indian idea of a university.

It is difficult to define precisely what constitutes an ashram. Sometimes it is confused with a *matha,* or monastery. The Ramakrishna order which began in 1897 originally called their mother house *Belur Matha*, but later the houses of the Ramakrishna order came to be known as ashrams. Ashrams are mentioned in ancient Indian literature, in particular the epics such as the *Ramayana*, where we hear of forest sages living in ashrams and it was they who welcomed the exiled warriors Rama and Lakshmana. The *Dharma Shastras*, or Hindu canons in which the ideals of Hindu life are outlined, speak of four *ashramas* or stages of life to which, ideally, every individual's biography should conform. Thus we have the ashramas of *Brahmachari* (student life), *Grihastha* (married life as a householder), *Vanaprastha* (wandering life in the forest, as a pilgrim) and finally *Sanyasa* (monkhood). The ashram, unlike the monastery in the western tradition, need not necessarily be the dwelling of celibate monks, though Gandhi felt that even married couples living together in an ashram should take a vow of celibacy.

The ashrams were characterised as schools for learning and also places which offered hospitality. The door of an ashram, according to one text, should always be open. The system of ashramas is also known as *Varnasramadharma*, that is, living according to the *Dharma* of both the *Varnas*, which is understood in the sense of vocational calling and *ashramas*, that is, stages of life. This close connection between the ashram concept and the idea of the *varnas* the literal meaning is "colour", has meant that many modern Indian Christians have felt that the ashram has been too much a part of the traditional Hindu caste system. Both Dalits, as well as Adivasis (tribals) have expressed a feeling of being alienated from the ashram pattern of life because they come from that part of Indian society which lies outside the caste system. In his autobiography, Gandhi decribes his radical move to include Dalit families in Satyagraha Ashram, Ahmedabad as early as 1916 and the storm this action provoked.

The modern mystic and philosopher, Sri Aurobindo, started an ashram in Pondicherry in 1910. He understood an ashram to be a place where people are called to follow a particular *Sadhana*, or spiritual search. In India, the idea of *Sadhana* overlaps with vocation, in the sense of the work or social duty which one is called upon to perform. Musicians, artists and dancers among other crafts people are supposed to follow a *sadhana*, rendering their work into a means towards finding God. *Bhakti* mystics like the great medieval theologian Ramanuja, developed a *Sadhana* philosophy, insisting that mystical insights can be found among people of different professions, all professions being understood in this sense as vocations.

"The institution of the asrama, was eventually adopted by every major religious sect, whether in the form of Vihara or Matha. In the structure of power, the King in his Kingdom and the ascetic in his exile, became counter-weights, one embedded in duties, obligations and rights, and the other emancipated from these." (Romila Thapar lecture on "Exile and Kingdom" at Mythic Society, Bangalore, 1978 p.25)

The ashrams are described in the Ramayana as places where the exiled king could discover a new type of order, even in the forest. It is this link between the ashram and *Ram Rajya,* or kingdom of God as Gandhi understood it, which made him use the ashram symbol as a way of emphasising a new kind of social order which can be discovered even through a type of political exile. The ashram is set over and against the corrupt centre of power as an ethical kingdom which is not concerned with worldly values but with the ultimate way of perfection. For Gandhi, the ashram became a centre for his *Sarvodaya* movement and his programme of village reconstruction.

As in Europe where monastic establishments played a vital role in preserving a tradition, the ashrams took on the role of educating the populace in the basic tenets of *Sanskritic* culture. The very epics may well have been written down and preserved from a vast ocean of story telling in these ashrams. The various dance schools and traditions of folk theatre and popular story telling even through images have been cultivated in such ashram centres, under the guidance of a *guru*.

(above) Simple lines of the Edaikodu Ashram. Photo: James Tombeur
(below) Tribal church in Zankhva, North Gujarat where the church is based in the house of the village chief. Photo: Sanjay

We are particularly concerned in this study with the way the ashram style of life has influenced the built space. In a way, the ashram is almost the antithesis of formal architecture, in the same way that the ashram is contrasted to the palace. In the ashram an attempt is made to simplify buildings so that only the essential is retained. Some have suggested that the very term ashram derives from ashraya meaning a shelter. What constitutes shelter? Certainly not elaboration of details or decoration. A return to basic needs is the complete opposite of the over-elaborate architecture which went by the name of Indo Saracenic, described in the chapter on orientalism. Architectural styles as a kind of dressing is, in this ashram context, stripped aside.

The ashram does, however, represent an attitude towards space and the relationship of building to the surrounding world of nature. In the Buddhist period of Indian architecture the forest retreat, or thatched wooden or bamboo hut, served as a model for the monastic shrine as we can see in the so-called "sketches" which have been carved out of solid rock on the Mahaballipuram shore in the fifth to sixth centuries. Here we can see the Indian crafts person experimenting with various architectural forms, which originated in simple wooden structures, to create a new kind of temple architecture, now made out of stone.

Looking back to the early history of church architecture in Europe, we can identify certain built forms coming from pre-Christian times which were adapted for church use.

First was the typical house church of the Middle East, found for example at Dura Europos on the Euphrates, where a central atrium or enclosed courtyard, with rooms leading from it, was taken as a model for a church before Christianity became the official religion of the Roman state. As this was also a time when Christians were persecuted, and important persons of the early church were martyred, the ancient model of the martyrium, or memoria, was used.

When Christianity was established as a state religion and assumed the various trappings of an earlier cult linked to the emperor, the basilica or hall, in which the emperor (basileus) or his agent presided, was made into the architectural prototype for the cathedral, or important parish church. The fact that these pre-Christian architectural forms were adopted by the early church suggest that other models of sacred buildings could also serve in shaping the form of the church, especially in India.

Other archetypal forms have given rise to what we now know as the Indian temple. There was the small shrine on a raised platform, often built under a tree, sometimes referred to as a *samadhi*, where the spirits of the ancestors and the vegetation (yakshas and yakshis) were venerated in folk culture. These small shrines can be found in the Indian countryside today and are often associated with fertility rites, taking the form of an enclosed structure built around a stone, or termite hill, or simply at the foot of a venerable and sacred tree. Here we see the origin of the later *Garba griha or Mulasthanam*, that is the womb house or root place, from which the whole temple complex is seen to evolve.

Another model for the sacred place in India has been the enclosed space whose high walls give the impression of a kind of fortress *(Durg)*. In fact, one of the most ancient deities in the popular pantheon is the female goddess called Durga, who was originally the guardian of the fortified settlement and was also associated with the enclosed area in which ancient tribal communities in India kept their cattle. Cows or buffaloes, represented the wealth of the community and all over the south of India there are memorial stones known as *Virakal* or hero stones, commemorating battles in which hero figures stood out against cattle thieves. Probably from these figures emerged the understanding of God as a herdsman protecting the animals who are also the souls (*anima*) of the faithful. Carl Jung has noted the link between the Latin word *animalis* meaning animal and *animus* meaning soul. Animals have often been used in societies to represent the souls of the faithful.

Enclosed fortified places in which animals were herded together for protection have been held to be sacred among various pastoral tribes such as the Todas in South India and have served as prototypes for a temple form where we find high walls surrounding an inner space with great doors leading in, known as gopuram meaning enclosed space of the cattle. The temple as a cattle shed also has its links with the ashram where we find a tendency to keep cattle as part of the life-style of the inmates. In popular imagination, the deity is called *Gopala*, keeper of the cows, or *Pasupatti*, lord of the animals. The cattle shed or barn has its own architectural features, which can relate to ashram architecture for example in the inner courtyard with the inward facing rooms.

Finally, there is the pillared hall which, like the basilica, was a meeting place for tribal chiefs and is known as a *mandapam*. Such halls, often built on high plinths, are a common feature of temple architecture and have been adapted in a number of churches. These halls served as places where pilgrims can rest, with facilities for preparing food called *bhojanalayas*, nearby Here also performances of mystery plays called *puranas*, epic narratives or myths, were enacted for the edification of the faithful. Another way of understanding the ashram setting is to view it as an open-air stage, which it often was. Kalakshetra near Madras has been conceived as a series of small dance halls, with a central open space dominated by a great banyan tree where performances can be staged. It is a typical setting which has much in common with the ashram tradition.

Rabindranath Tagore tried to create a kind of ashram architecture in Shantiniketan. A good example of this was the house he created for himself and lived in during the last years of his life which he called *syamali*. (Syamali means the earth as dark, beauteous and green). Here we see a mud building reminiscent of the Santali tribal villages still seen around Shantiniketan. The houses are built from compressed clay, following ancient techniques which use heavy outside walls that tend to slope gradually inwards and often have an upper loft below a rather dome-like bamboo roof structure thatched with straw. Inside partitions are woven bamboo work sometimes plastered over with a thin layer of clay to make a kind of wattled wall. The

Shantiniketan, Kala Bhavan, showing the mud huts with wall decorations in the Santali style which had influenced Rabindranath Tagore.

general impression of *syamali* is that of a rather rustic *vihara*, a Buddhist monastery which may well have its architectural prototypes in the village structures of nearby Bihar. Village building techniques and styles would provide an appropriate way of viewing ashram architecture.

Gandhi experimented with a kind of ashram architecture, especially at Wardha in the Sevagram Ashram which was his main base towards the end of his life. The mud-built rooms which he occupied and used for his meetings can still be seen. They have a number of low mud reliefs decorating the walls which are very reminiscent of the wall decoration found among tribal houses of central India. Gandhi said :

> "I believe that if India is to attain true freedom and through India the world as well, then sooner or later we will have to live in villages - in huts, not in palaces. A few billion people can never live happily and peaceably in cities" (Gandhi in a letter to J. Nehru in "Hind Swaraj" 1908).

Architects like Laurie Baker have been eloquent about the virtues of mud or brick buildings. Various churches which he designed are built of unplastered brick because it is low cost and has aesthetic value. He had a deep appreciation of the beauty of Indian villages and has even pointed out that the kind of structures which villagers put up in cities, and which are called slums, have a value of their own, and should not just be dismissed as eyesores. Those who care to look at such simple homes will find they are often constructed with great care using, to the very best advantage, limited space and building materials which are often thrown away and are, therefore, almost free. If architecture is about using space and materials economically, then traditional village architecture should be our model if we want to imagine a future where most will have the possibility of having a home of their own.

Such concerns inspired those who advocate the ashram as a way of life which is respectful of the environment and not

The chapel of Christava Ashram, Manganam, Kerala
designed by Laurie Baker.
The roof is modelled on the typical conical
roof of village temples in Kerala.

wasteful with materials. If orientalists were concerned primarily with external appearance and lavish decoration, indianisers wanted to find more typical features which would incarnate the gospel within the Indian cultural ethos.

The ashram movement was concerned, above all, with a style of life. There is no point worshipping in an artificially created church in an Indian style when the worshippers afterwards revert to a style of life which has nothing to do with the forms that they try to imitate when at prayer. Why sit on the floor in church when you would never think of sitting on the floor at home? Why use oil lamps in church when oil lamps are never used at home? Why take off your shoes, when everywhere else footwear is the norm? These were the sort of questions which the ashram seekers raised. The ashram is not just an institution but a whole attitude to life. It is this demand for consistency, a sense of the sacred emanating from the ordinary and day-to-day rather than imposed from above as something exotic, that is the basic character which ashram buildings represent.

This is not just utilitarianism. When poets and artists like those who gathered around Tagore tried to create a style of art close to ordinary people, they were not just doing this in order to go back to the past and reject modernity simply because it was new. Rather, they felt that a sense of the beauty of simple materials and a culture close to nature has an enduring quality that has been lost touch of with much that is modern. Some have called this approach post-modern. Certainly, even in the west, modern artists and architects are going back to what might be called the basic function of art: not to make something which is artificial and contrary to nature but rather to discover the essential forms of nature and create a culture out of these forms.

Because the ashram ideal embraces every aspect of life, the ashram as a model for the church in India does not provide only a place for worship. For Gandhi, the ashram provided the locus for the total transformation of Indian society. The ashram, as he saw it, is an educational institution and a model for the wider community. Certainly, going back to ancient times the *gurukula*, or family of the *guru*, was pictured in an ashram setting. This was a kind of education not limited to book learning. Education took place through a shared life with people who had experience and could communicate that experience in an existential way. Tagore, Gandhi, Aurobindo, and J. Krishnamurthy all tried to find ways of revitalising the Indian education system using, as their inspiration, a return to the *gurukula* system. When, in 1934, a small group of idealistic young people, mainly from the Mar Thoma branch of the Syrian Christian Church, started a home and school for homeless children in Aleppey, their hopes were quite modest and practical. They wanted to provide an education for those whom society had rejected. This education should be not only academic but should also be what might be called technical. So when the group, led by Acharya Chandy, shifted to Manganam near Kottayam, a printing press and workshops for other crafts were established. On a plot of land of about eight acres, various activites which include agricultural work engaged the ashramites. Their prospectus, states: "Started in 1958, the Ashram Gurukul helps educate young men and women who, in an atmosphere of prayer, study, productive work and life together in the Ashram community, get a vision of the Kingdom of God".

Another type of Ashram is more concerned with spiritual search than with good works. This distinction between contemplative and active, which has plagued Christian spirituality in the west, has not actually been a concern in Indian thought. So Richard Taylor's distinction between *khadi* ashrams, those following the active ministry which Gandhi envisaged, and *kavi* ashrams where a contemplative life in the tradition of the Vedic *Rishis* is attempted, again makes a feature out of external forms - the clothes which are worn, for example. But the ashram ideal, as pointed out earlier, has always been holistic.

The ashram has been understood as a place for healing. In ancient times ashrams were connected with the *Siddhas*, who

The Christu Kula Ashram front gate or gopuram.
(opposite) Interior altar (photos: Ken Hassell).

were the Indian equivalent of alchemists in that their practical or scientific interests combined with a spiritual search for transformation. When the two doctors Savarirayan Jesudasan and Ernest Forrester Paton, who had been connected with the Vellore Christian Medical College, felt called to go and work amongst the villages, they decided to establish an ashram which they called the Christu Kula Ashram. Explaining what had attracted him to the ashram ideal, Dr. Jesudasan writes :

> "As the inmates of these ashrams dwelt in forest and depended for their physical sustenance upon what grew around them they also began to study the herbs and their healing properties. This developed a certain kind of research in medical science and they developed systems of therapy, for example the Siddha system of medicine. To this extent the ancient ashrams served as centres of scientific research. (Savarirayan Jesudasan, *"Ashrams, Ancient and Modern"* p.6 pub: Sri Ramachandra Press, Vellore 1937).

Both Fr Monchanin at Shantivanam Ashram and Verrier Elwin at the Christa Prema Seva Ashram in Pune imitated already existing temple structures when it came to designing a

Anjali Ashram Chapel under Chamundi Hill, Mysore.
(below) Interior showing the altar (vedi) and tomb (Samadhi)
of Fr Amalapavoradas.
(interior photo: Caroline Mackenzie)

chapel for their Ashram. According to Sister Barbara Noreen in her unpublished study of Christa Seva Sangh (A Wheat Grain Sown in India" 1988), Verrier Elwin a member of the Ashram constructed a prayer shrine near a small stream shielded by a clump of trees.

> "It was designed and the building largely carried out by Keshav and Stanley and was one of the first serious experiments in putting Indian architecture to Christian use for the purpose of worship. It was built in the style of a small Hindu temple. Carol Graham describes it as the replica of a local temple. William Paton remarked that it was an exact copy of one of the shrines which were 'pilgrim resting places' and which were a familiar sight on the great pilgrim routes." (Noreen "A Wheat Grain Sown in India" op cit 91)

Unfortunately this original Mandir (temple structure) no longer exists, though a sketch of it is seen in Angela da Fonseca's fresco in the Ashram prayer room. At the time of construction there was some controversy:

> "... there was a certain amount of criticism and trepidation about this small temple built in 'Hindu' style. The Brothers pointed out that it had always been the custom of the church to take over the architecture of the countries into which it had spread, consecrating it to Christian use. They cited the example of the Pantheon in Rome and the small ruined church of St Pancras in the grounds of St Augustine's college at Canterbury." (Noreen op cit p.91)

However even so sympathetic adviser as William Paton felt it was "outdated" and pointed out that modern Indians were trying to "shed the signs of their old religious superstitions". Close friends and frequent visitors to the Ashram, Dr Forrester-Paton and Dr Jesudasan planned to build a temple in the

Christu Kula Ashram but this is now in danger of being dismantled because of a growing sense of unease about churches built in a Hindu pattern. A temple church in South Arcot is currently used as a class-room.

The effort of Fr Monchanin to build the chapel of Shantivanam Ashram on the model of a Shiva temple (chap 4) was related to attempts to make an Indian type of liturgy and also to discover an Indian spirituality. At the Anjali Ashram also, Fr Amalorpavadas took regular courses in Indian spirituality which included techniques of meditation and yogic exercises.

There is a relationship between the ashram and the practice of yoga. The term *yoga*, which is related to the word yoke, is understood by Sri Aurobindo as integration. Fr. Bede Griffiths, who was very much impressed by the ideas of Sri Aurobindo, suggested that at the centre of the ashram pattern of life there should be the practice of some form of yoga. For this purpose a circular hall was built for yoga and meditation at Shantivanam Ashram, at the centre of which an image of Jesus in meditation, facing the four points of the compass, was installed.

Finally, the ashram was also conceived of as a place which could provide hospitality to wandering pilgrims. It is a place and yet it is also not a fixed institution. The ashram, like the pilgrim, has a tendency to move where the guru goes and so is itself part of the journey. This characterises the way in which an ashram like the Christa Prema Seva Ashram in Pune has evolved. Father Bill Lash, who was for some years the *acharya* of this ashram writes that the patron of the ashram is St. Francis of Assisi and though they aim at serving the sick and the poor, the way they have been able to follow this calling is by "giving temporary shelter to wayfaring men". This mendicant life, which was what St. Francis also embraced, is certainly close to the spirituality of India. Sr Sara Grant has described how the *Varkaris,* who are wandering devotees of Lord Krishna at the pilgrimage centre of Pandapur, often come to rest a while on the open verandahs which surround an inner garden space of the ashram. Here we find a mingling of traditional Christian spirituality and *Bhakti* or devotional tradition to be found in India. The idea of an enclosed garden space with a small shrine in the centre, situated under a tree and surrounded by rooms opening inwards onto a verandah space, is ideally suited to this vocation of providing a resting place for wanderers. Unfortunately, the growing city of Pune has now engulfed this peaceful spot and high rise buildings are expected to come up all around what was a sheltered corner. The future of the ashram is in question and many who helped to found it have had to move on, finding themselves to be pilgrims like those whom they tried to welcome to the ashram.

Perhaps in the modern world the ashram has to change. It is not possible to cling to the past. There are many critics of the ashram today and a large number are having to close down. The ashram was not just an institution, a cluster of buildings more or less permanent. It was also a way of understanding the universe and the relation of the human person to that universe. Taken seriously, the ashram did present a very different concept of ecclesia, one which was in harmony with the spirit of India. The ashram movement has been of great interest to young seekers from the west, though Indian Christians have increasingly felt disenchanted. We will have to look more deeply into the reasons for this disenchantment in the second half of this book. But the Ashram, by stressing what is essential and permanent in the human quest for God, can never really become out of date. We only have to look for new ways in which its relevance for the future can be realised.

Shiva Temple at Magadipattu in Pondicherry State was the "model" on
which Fr Monchanin based his dream
of the ideal chapel for Shantivanam Ashram (page 81f).

6

Church Building as Teaching Aid

The sacred building does not just provide shelter. It is also an image of reality and, as such, is a revelation in the same way that the holy book communicates the divine word of God. The temple or church is understood as a statement but in a different sense from the word we find in a book. It is the image that is revealed. In ancient religious thought, whether biblical or vedic, word and image are not understood as two distinct realities but are seen as representing two facets of the same primordial and creative truth. In India, where the majority of the population even to this day remain illiterate, it is the visual form, image, sculpture or building which is the primary means for transmitting cultural and spiritual meanings.

When worshippers go to a temple or a church, they learn something about the nature of faith. The building has a narrative function: it tells a story, and the story can be in the form of mythological or symbolic scenes which are depicted on the walls of the holy place. The architecture of the religious edifice is designed to provide a structure in which the image can be seen. But not only images are displayed on the walls of the building, words, too, have contributed to the decoration of wall spaces. In Islamic architecture the flowing forms of Arabic script help us to understand not only the Koran but also the way in which the mosque itself has evolved. The proportions of the mosque, its cursive character with the long stroke of the vertical minarets, and its linear rhythms seen in the arches, domes and other features of the built form, indicate that the building itself is like a beautiful piece of calligraphy.

The building is, in a certain sense, something written on the landscape, like a word written on the page of a book. It is also like a kind of vessel or instrument through which the spoken word of the holy book is made audible to the community. Not only is the voice of the *Muezzin* made audible by the height of the minarets but the very domes which span the inner spaces of the mosque help to contain the words of the preacher. They become like the sounding box of a carefully tuned musical instrument, a means to contain sound and carry it to the listening ears of the faithful. Architecture, especially sacred architecture, is intended to help the faithful hear the word of God and to enlarge or amplify their songs of praise. In that way, the built form is visual music, to be heard as much as seen. Chanting is particularly suited to architectural spaces. It is almost as though the proportions and acoustics of the sacred building are the natural extension of the human voice, giving a new dimension to the power of utterance.

Many of the experimental churches in India are in some way connected with *theologates*, or places for religious instruction. The building is itself a teaching aid. In the large, modern, marble-clad temple of Tulsimanasa Mandir in Varanasi the entire Ramayana of Tulsidas is written on the walls. For the benefit of those who cannot read, the temple is also arranged like a stage, the whole epic being presented in the form of scenes with puppets at which the faithful can look and discuss the various events depicted. In the Middle Ages, the great cathedrals were also conceived of as the "Bible of the poor", which is what St. Bernard of Clairvaux wanted them to be. The stained glass windows, the tapestries and carved representations of the saints all present a rich array of visual forms which heighten the consciousness of the worship to a point where visiting the holy place is like entering another dimension of reality, almost dream-like in its symbolic intensity.

The church as a seminary bridges the gap between the

ashram and the cathedral. In recent times there has been an effort in India to revitalise theological training by making it more contextual. The result has been the creation of regional theologates, or centres for religious and spiritual training, where not only book learning goes on but the whole personality of the individual seeker is addressed through a pattern of life which prepares the student for Christian ministry.

An example of such an experimental approach to religious education is the Tamilnadu Theological Seminary in Madurai. Founded in an ancient centre of Tamil culture and learning, the college has attempted to integrate its students with a cultural milieu which extends far beyond the walls of the seminary compound. The whole campus has been thought out creatively with the help of architect Laurie Baker, who conceived of a seminary as a lived space where the interaction between teachers and students and their whole style of life, is reflected in the buildings.

The chapel at Tamilnadu is a pillared space
opening into an enclosed garden.

Tamilnad Theological Seminary
(sketch K.G. Mathew)
(right) Metal relief of Christ as a
Pandavan King made by
Cheldurai

Perhaps his inspiration was partly a Gandhian type of ashram, as attempted at the famous Gandhigram near Madurai. But the seminary, dedicated as much to the service of the community as to the serious study of theology, was planned as a kind of sermon in brick. Laurie Baker felt that the very rough unplastered bricks used had much to say about the relationship between ordinary life and a spiritual ideal. The chapel is meant to be understood not just as a building in itself but as part of the whole campus. The way in which the chapel opens out onto the campus and yet has its own enclosed space helps to give it a character of being both a special place and a place integrated with the whole life of the community. The rather informal atmosphere found in this chapel has helped it to be used as a place for experimental liturgies which try to address

The altar at Sambalpur Regional Seminary with mosaic by Jyoti Sahi of Jesus washing the feet of the disciples.

Carved wooden doors at Sambalpur Regional Seminary represent Jesus and Mary as dancers.
(right) Grill design representing the Cosmic Drum as source of sound (the Word).
Design: Jyoti Sahi.

social issues in which the college is very much engaged and for which this seminary is now well-known.

Another attempt at a regional seminary has been the building of the Kristo Jyoti Vidyalaya at Sambalpur in Orissa. This seminary has been planned to serve the need of five dioceses in Orissa, where the majority of Christians come from either a Dalit or Adivasi background. Though Orissa, as a state of India, has the largest proportion of Adivasi and Dalit communities of any state in India, it is also renowned for its fine cultural traditions linked to the great temple of Lord Jaganath in Puri. The history of the regional culture of Orissa is very complex. The whole discussion on the relationship between what some scholars in the past termed the "little" traditions and the "great" Sanskritic or classical tradition of the Hindu synthesis, has given rise in Orissa to a new awareness of distinctive regional cultures (Jyoti Sahi *Seeds of Tradition* in "Dharma" 1998). There is a particular amalgamation of cultural streams creating what many are now studying as the emergence of a regional culture.

This gives rise to something in between the very localised and largely oral cultures of wandering tribes people and the pan-Indian, highly Sanskritised literary cultures linked to the Vedanta.

In the regional theologate a similar attempt is made to find a bridge between a universalistic faith system, what the theologian Aloysius Pieris calls a metacosmic religion, and localised forms of popular spirituality which are cosmic and earth-centred.

Another regional theologate has been established at Sameeksha, a unique ashram-seminary which has been created by Fr. Sebastian Painadath at Kalady. Here, by the side of a river within a grove of trees, where a cluster of houses have been built in a simple style, young men from Kerala study theology in a gur*ukul* environment. Just down the river are Hindu *mutts* (monasteries) marking the place where the famous Adi Shankaracharya was born in the ninth century of the Christian Era. Fr. Sebastian is an expert in the Sanskrit language and has made a deep study of the Bhagavad Gita. He often gives Gita retreats for Christians to help familiarise them with one of the most important spiritual texts which serve as the gospel for most educated Hindus.

The ashram prayer or meditation hall is an open space where different holy books - Hindu and Muslim, as well as Christian scriptures - are left open for those who wish to study them. At the centre is a lamp. The doors face outwards to the four points of the compass and in the garden around are various cosmic symbols which are also related to the elements. A large stone cut lamp of the type common in front of Keralian temples reminds one of the importance of light in all religious traditions.

The building of churches in an Indian style has been determined by efforts to create an Indian liturgy using elements derived from temple worship. When the National Biblical, Catechetical and Liturgical Centre at Bangalore was commissioned in 1967 to look into the relationship of the post-Vatican Council church to Indian culture, the chapel was an integral part of its teaching programme. The chapel was designed in the early 1970's with the inspiration of Fr Amalorpavadas who wanted to make the Indian rite liturgy central to the spiritual life of the Centre. The chapel was designed on the ground plan of the ancient Vedi, or sacrificial fire altar, which is supposed to represent a bird in flight with outstretched wings. In one of these wings is situated the Indian-type altar at which the priest sits cross-legged on the ground. The *Vimanam* (head) of the structure is located directly opposite the entrance and provides the setting for the tabernacle in the form of a symbolic pillar which represents the axis of the universe.

One of the oldest centres for learning is Varanasi on the banks of the Ganges. There, for millennia, sages have gathered from different parts of India, both to learn and to teach. Every school of thought to be found in India has its representatives in this ancient city which is, in essence, like a university town. In recent times, the Benares Hindu University was established on the outskirts of this city to continue the tradition of learning in this place. On another extremity of the city is Sarnath,

(above) Interior of NBCLC Chapel showing the Cosmic Pillar
(below) Sameeksha Ashram meditation room with scriptures facing all points of the compass.

The chapel of the National Biblical, Catechetical and Liturgical Centre in Bangalore.

The sketch shows the structure of the chapel based on the form of the vedi (an ancient vedic fire altar).

(opposite ⇨)

Octagonal chapel at Mathridam Ashram, Christnagar, Varanasi.
(photo I.M.S.)

where the Lord Buddha preached his first sermon to a small group of disciples. There are many Buddhist institutions where Buddhist monks continue to teach their scriptures.

At Christ Nagar near Varanasi, where the Indian Missionary Society has set up its headquarters, an ashram called Matridham was established in 1954. From 1955-56 the ashram acted as the novitiate, or house of formation, for the Indian Missionary Society. A group of about twenty simple mud huts were grouped in the form of the petals of a lotus flower and it was here that the young aspirants to religious life received their first initiation into Indian spirituality.

Later, Swami Ishwar Prasad of the Indian Missionary Society took over the ashram, which had fallen into disuse, and gave it new impetus in 1983. People came for courses in Indian spirituality and a chapel was constructed at the centre of the ashram. This is basically an octagonal structure, rather like the ancient Syrian baptistries. On one side, a niche-like apsidal extension serves as a *garbha griha* where the tabernacle is mounted in a pillar setting.

This Ashram now has become the centre for a largely lay movement, where many local villagers gather to receive instruction not only in religious matters but also spiritual healing. The present acharya, Fr. Anil Dev, has a charismatic understanding of ashram life, combining in the ashram two traditional functions of such centres for community living. One is a teaching function and the other a healing one. He claims that up to 1500 *khrista bhaktas* are in the habit now of visiting this ashram, where *sat sanghs,* gatherings of the saints, take place for hours together. During these *sat sangh* meetings, people from surrounding villages are instructed in the basics of Indian spirituality as understood from a Christian perspective. Informal prayers, bhajans and healings take place. Those who come to the ashram are not necessarily Christian.

There are Hindus who feel very doubtful about the evangelical thrust which certain Christian ashrams are assuming. The ashram as a place where spirituality courses are conducted and sermons given means that the Christian ashram assumes a different character from what it earlier stood for: expressing gospel values through a way of life rather than through words. The ashram as a means of teaching people about the way in which the Christian gospel can be inculturated can easily become propagandist, a kind of technique for evangelisation. In the present climate of growing fundamentalism, in Christian circles as well as in Hindu and Muslim, dialogue as a way of understanding the other, becomes subservient to an evangelical desire to convert the other. Here lies one of the basic ambiguities of the inculturation movement which has been much debated in recent years. Theologians like Fr. Michael Amalados have spoken of mission as dialogue but this becomes increasingly difficult in an atmosphere of distrust, where even the effort to take on the cultural patterns of another religious tradition and use their symbols is perceived as a way of taking over believers and proselytising them. Christians have been accused of assuming Hindu manners and customs simply in order to gain converts. In such an atmosphere, inculturation works against dialogue, not for it. The missionary is thought to intrude into the sacred space of another spiritual tradition, not as a friend or guest but as an invader.

We face an ontological problem: the tension between being and having, between the disinterested desire to share and understand the other and the interested intention to gain control over or possess the other. Certainly, mission in India will have to develop a theology of the "other", for which currently there is no adequate understanding. Dr. Raimundo Panikkar, who lived many years in the ambience of the *ghats* of Varanasi, struggled in different ways to understand how the Christian might remain open to truth claims of other religious traditions while remaining faithful to an inner commitment to Christ. Those who live and teach in a place like Varanasi cannot ignore the diversity of spiritual experience and the need for something more than just religious tolerance.

That I may ever be at the service of Thy love
Give me Lord, union with Thee
(Ashram sloka antiphon)

7

The Prayer Room

The prayer room could be described as the most primal form of church. The earliest churches were probably house churches, like the upper room where Jesus and his disciples first gathered to share the last supper together. It was in a Jewish home, in a room set aside for receiving honoured guests like a rabbi, where Jesus and his disciples ate their last meal together that the church began. Later, it was probably a similar room, if not the same one, where the disciples continued to gather and where Jesus appeared to them after his death. Finally, it was undoubtedly in such a room, probably in an upper room, that the assembled disciples experienced the outpouring of the Holy Spirit on the feast of Pentecost.

In every traditional Indian home a portion of the house, if possible even a small room, is set aside to hold the family shrine. In simple village homes this shrine for the household deity is often located in the kitchen area but in bigger, wealthier establishments such a shrine within the home would have its own space, which is like the *garbha griha* that we find in the temple.

In the houses of some religious communities, particularly of congregations which are concerned to discover an Indian form of spirituality, it is now quite common to find a prayer room. This prayer room replaces the earlier chapels which were set aside in every house of a religious order for the devotions of the community. In many ways a prayer room is used just like a chapel but the difference is that it is used not only for eucharistic liturgies but is also a quiet place where people come to pray. In Catholic institutions these prayer rooms often contain a tabernacle in which the Eucharist is reserved and becomes a focus for meditation. In some orders, for example the little Sisters of Jesus or the Little Brothers of Jesus, who are inspired by the spirituality of Brother Charles de Foucauld, there is the tradition of exposing the blessed sacrament in a special vessel, traditionally known as a monstrance but now sometimes simply placed in some kind of vessel where it can be seen and meditated upon This devotion to the body of Christ not to be shared in the form of a meal but just seen as in the Hindu idea of *darshana* is a particularly Roman Catholic tradition.

Chapel of Yesu Ashram (Little Sisters of Jesus) Kamanahalli, Bangalore

There have been a number of attempts to construct prayer rooms where inter-faith dialogue can be done in a prayerful context. The prayer room at Ashirvad, Bangalore was originally intended as a centre for inter-faith dialogue and is structured on the basic Buddhist Yin-Yang symbol to represent the interflow of light and dark principles in creation.

In the Brahmin area of Bangalore, the prayer room of the Daughters of the Church congregation uses the symbol of the tree of life carried through in a low altar which is a pillar surmounted by a tabernacle in the form of a full vessel of life. This idea of having a place where an individual can feel alone with God to reflect on the holy scriptures is also finding increasing favour among some Protestant communities particularly in a hospital or a school. A number of Christian hospitals have a room set aside for those who want to pray, especially the sick or the relatives and friends of some person who is in particular need of support through prayer.

The designing of such prayer rooms requires an approach to sacred space different from that which we find in a church, where the space is planned to hold a congregation presided over by officiating ministers who perform certain rituals for the faithful. The prayer room is not really intended as a ritual space in that sense. Rather, it is a space which helps in the cultivation of an inner spirituality and a sense of calm interiority. The word "interiority" has become a key word in the practice of different forms of Indian spirituality, such as *yoga*, or *prana yama* (discipline of breathing) and *dhyana* (meditation techniques). The repetition of the name of God or some key phrase of the Bible and the singing of *bhajans* are other aspects of the activities for which the prayer room is suited.

Often the prayer room invites Christians to experiment with Indian forms of ritual which are different from those which are acceptable within the church. An example of this is the ritual of *arathi*, the offering of lights and other symbols of the earth as a sign of welcoming the presence of God the Spirit, or the incarnate Lord, into the home. In many traditional Indian homes the housewife decorates the door-step of the home, and also the door of the prayer room, with patterns known as *kolama, rangoli* or *alpana*. These patterns symbolise the gesture of welcoming the deity into the home. This popular devotion derives originally from the ritual of the mandala, where the divine presence is invoked within a circular design. In the past, Christians have tended to avoid using such patterns or decorating the door of the home in any special way, feeling that these were pagan superstitions. In Kerala, however, in the traditional home of a Syrian Christian, we find a central storeroom, known as the *ara* where the precious grains or other crops which the Christians often traded found a safe keeping. This *ara* often has a decorated door. In front of this door in the evening a lamp is sometimes lit around which the family gathers for prayers.

The understanding of the home as a sacred space is the basis for the canonical books known as the *Vastu Shastras* or, in Kerala the *Thakku Shastras*, the *thakkan* being the traditional master carpenter, or *achari*. Going back to ancient tribal times, the home is pictured as a microcosm. The carpenter/architect not only builds the home but also consults the stars for an auspicious time to begin and observes the general lay of the land on which the house has to be built. The relation of the house to sources of water like a well in the land where it is built is vital. A temple, which is the house of a god, must never be built on land which has no source of water nearby. The building is married to the land and is understood as masculine, in that it is conceived of ideally as the body of a man, *purusha*. The land is the wife. The term *purusha* is popularly applied to a husband who is spoken of as the sacrificer, *yajman*.

Because the house is a person, not simply a thing, it has to be treated as something living. The house has openings like the human body, and what is good and nourishing to this body enters through one door, while what is polluting and dead, leaves by another door. For example, guests and important articles needed for the sustaining of the home should come in through the front door, whereas all refuse and things which might pollute the home, are taken out through the back door. The housewife does not sweep towards the front door but towards the back door. Visitors take their shoes off when entering the home. Where people sit, eat or sleep, all is planned out according to an underlying symbolic picture of the ideal home. The kitchen with its grinding stone and hearth, the prayer room with its little throne on which the image of the household deity is placed, all have their proper place.

In modern times the home has become secularised and, especially amongst Christians, there is a tendency to disregard all these rituals of the home. In rural places, the habit of looking after the home in a particular way continues. In recent times, there has been a great revival of interest in the *Vasthu Shastras* and many Hindus are careful to follow the basic principles set out in these canons of architecture. So much so, that a new centre for the study of these canons has been established in Kerala and many professional architects in India have been studying them. As far as I know, no homes of religious communities among Christians have consciously thought about the sacred meaning of the house.

If the home is sacralised, time is also an important aspect of the ritual of life. In Indian thought there are sacred times known as *sandhyas* which are supposed to represent the meeting of light and darkness, inner and outer. Dawn and dusk are important *sandhyas*, although mid-day is also thought of as a *sandhya* since that is the time the sun changes its ascending course up to the heavens and begins to descend once more to the horizon. Some have defined the sacred as a point of transition, of moving from one plane of existence to another. There are many such points of transition in the life of an individual which are known as *samskaras*. The time of birth, first taking of solid food, first walking, puberty, marriage, going out of the home on some important journey, returning home, sickness and death, are all *samskaras* and the rituals associated with these times of transition are expressed in terms of gestures which point to the inner significance of the home. The doorway, as a transition from inner to outer, is treated with special reverence as is the door-step leading from the outer level of the street up to the plinth level of the house floor.

Inculturation implies an acceptance of a total understanding of life as a blessing and an incarnation of gospel values into cultural ways of expressing those values. Hindus have tended to criticise Christian efforts at inculturation as being half-hearted, often concerned only with externals and not really looking to the inner spirit or meaning behind outer forms. An example would be the use of *arathi* as a way of blessing. The ritual gesture of *arathi* is found in all Indian forms of worship and is generally performed by the woman of the house, although the man as sacrificer also performs *arathi* as an act of consecration. There have been different efforts to explain the significance of this ritual, which consists of offering different symbolic elements, like fire, incense, flowers, fruits, and liquids. The offering is generally placed in a plate then waved with a circular, clockwise movement before the welcome guest, image, doorway or other object to be blessed.

One of the stories told in the Shri Vaishnavite tradition explains the origins of *arathi*. This story shows the link between *arathi* and the home as shelter or sacred place.

> In primordial times there were wandering on the earth inspired ascetics known as *alvars*, who were pilgrims as well as poets and seers. Once there was a terrible storm and in order to escape from the downpour, one of these *alvars* sought for shelter in a little shrine which he found beneath a tree. The shrine had only one door and was big enough for him to lie down. After a while, another *alvar* who was passing that way also came to the door of this shrine, seeking shelter from the storm. He entered and was made welcome but then there was only space for the two alvars to sit. Presently a third *alvar* who by some chance was also wandering in that place, came to the door of the shrine and asked to be admitted. Now there was space only for the three holy men to stand. In the darkness, with the door closed and standing close together, the saints began to discuss the feeling they shared that there was a fourth person also present. Who was this fourth person? They could not identify the presence. One of the mystics offered to make a small lamp out of some clay. Another offered to fill the lamp with some oil which he had with him. The third had fire and offered to create a light with this lamp. They then began

looking around the dark interior of the small shrine. At last, in the darkness they found the image or symbol of the divine in whose presence they had been taking shelter from the storm. (a traditional story told to the author by Sri Sounder Rajan)

This act of searching for, and finding, the divine image is said to be the origin of the ritual of *arathi*. Underlying the gesture of *arathi* is an understanding of sacred space as shelter but a space which is essentially mysterious and dark and which, like the cave, has to be explored. Light is brought into the darkness in order to reveal or unveil what is hidden. This is a process of going into the depths, of discovering what lies hidden within. An example of this is the chapel of the Trappist sisters in Mekiad, Kerala.

The idea of the upper room comes from a different cultural setting. In Middle Eastern homes, the room on the roof of the house set aside for the honoured guest was a room on another level, a room nearer to heaven which is conceived as being above. You have to ascend to enter this room. This room is associated with light rather than darkness. The symbolic

(left)
Carved entrance to the Chapel of the Trappist sisters, designed by Caroline Mackenzie.

Chapel of the Trappist sisters, Anand Matha, Wyanad, North Kerala design by Caroline Mackenzie.

movement of the church, as it was understood in its Semitic cultural context, was a process of ascent to the mountain of the Lord. Here, on this eschatological mountain, a light is set so all can see it. This is the significance of that parable of Jesus where he speaks of a lamp being set on a lamp stand and not hidden underneath a bushel. Brother Charles de Foucauld spoke of announcing the gospel from the roof-tops with his life. Here again, we have the typical middle eastern image of the home with its flat roof, onto which the holy man ascends to announce to all around his spiritual experience. In Islamic tradition, the m*uezzin* ascended to such a height to call the faithful to prayer and it is this which has gradually developed into the minaret.

The Hindu or Buddhist tradition has a different understanding of spiritual search. Here there is an effort to go downwards to the depths, to find the Lord hidden in the cave *(guha)* of the heart *(chid)*. Both contain a deep spiritual truth. But the image which the home expresses through two signs - of the inner womb house *(garbha griha)* without window at the centre of the house and the upper room of the Semitic tradition - are different perceptions of the sacred. The problem is, which does the inculturated church in India opt for? Can both symbols be combined into a new type of synthesis? Can the Indian church be a kind of mixture of both Hindu temple and Islamic mosque? Can the Christian in India affirm two cultures, one Semitic and the other Aryan or even Dravidian? Can the symbols derive from a cultural background of the open desert in central Asia as well as the tropical forest with its wild storms and downpours? Into which climate does the gospel naturally fit?

These questions cannot be answered easily and it has been a struggle for the church in India to find a solution to these deep cultural claims. Spirituality cannot just be other-worldly. Even the images we use for deep mystical insights are culturally conditioned. What is important about cultures is that they are not the same. There are profound differences and these differences represent the richness and variety of creation. Having accepted that there is something universal about the gospel, we also believe that this universal quality has to be found in the particular and the local.

A final image comes from Indian poet Rabindranath Tagore. He said once that he wanted his home to be filled with breezes coming from every side, with all the doors open. But, he cautioned "I do not want my home to be blown down". It is in that spirit that we are searching for the universal which, like the spirit, "comes from we know not where" but which was heard by the prophet Elijah in the cave as "a still small voice".

The two movements, one towards interiority and the other towards outer manifestation, provide a kind of axis which is not simply cultural but is to be found in all religious typologies. In the emergence of the early church we have two types of building, one, the *martyrium*, which evolved from a small structure called a *memorium*, often a shrine above the tomb of a specially revered and loved individual and, on the other hand, the *basilica*, which developed out of the official meeting hall which the Romans used for public occasions presided over by the Emperor or his agent. The martyrium tended to be more intimate and was either circular or octagonal in ground plan. The Basilica was a long hall, with side aisles culminating in a presidium at the apse end where the seat of the president was situated. It later developed into the throne of the bishop in the cathedral. In the early churches of the east, particularly Syria, the *martyrium* was much favoured, whereas the *basilica* came more and more to dominate in the west. In the Gothic synthesis, the two forms were combined by making the baptistry in the west front near the door, very much in the form of the earlier *martyriums*, often an octagonal structure, in an enclosed and more intimate type of space.

When Fr. Monchanin wanted to design a chapel in Shantivanam Ashram in Tamilnadu, he felt it would be important to have the *garbha griha*, or womb house as the *mulasthanam* of the temple *mandapam*. Fr. Le Saux, later called Swami Abhishiktananda, suggested an octagonal structure like that in the ancient *martyriums* but Fr. Monchanin objected that this was too Syrian (Letter written by Fr. Monchanin, Feb. 14, 1950). The *martyrium* had come to be associated with the baptistry and for Fr Monchanin the *garbha griha* should be the ultimate mystery of the Eucharist. Here the tabernacle would be installed for the reservation of the blessed sacrament. This would be in line with the tendency in the Indian rite, as developed later by Swami Abhishiktananda and Fr. Ignatius Irudayam on the lines of agamic ritual (canonical books referring to the rubrics of worship) and accepted by Fr. Amalorpavadas, as providing a form of Indian Eucharistic celebration in the way of a *puja*. In this *puja, arathi* is performed at three places: (a) welcoming the priest, (b) welcoming the worshippers, (c) welcoming the divine presence at the second elevation after the consecration.

The Rev. John Daniels, who earlier had done a careful study on "The Meanings of Hindu Puja: an exercise in Intentional Analysis" (1992), has recently written an essay particularly concerned with the Indian rite as performed at the National

Biblical Catechetical and Liturgical Centre entitled "Not Hinduization but Christianization: A Thematic Comparison of Hindu Puja and the Eucharist." He writes :

> "The recognition that contextual transition entails semantic difference is of central importance in evaluating the adoption of traditionally non-Christian symbols/ritual elements into Christian worship. In this study I have reviewed one of the paradigmatic themes found in Hindu puja and sought to elaborate its content. It emerges that some semantic overlap with the Christian tradition does indeed pertain. The task of the adaptor is therefore to build on the common "semantic kernel" in such a way as to minimize those elements of original meaning which are theologically incongruous in their new context and to maximise those novel elements which the symbol is to carry if it is to discharge a theologically valid function in its new setting."

The critical kernel of what he has to say lies in his analysis of the significance of guest/host relationships within the *puja*, where divinity is invited into the sacred space as a guest and, on the other hand, the Christian understanding of the Eucharist as host, where the Lord invites the worshippers to come and share in the divine banquet which he has prepared.

The place of Eucharist in Christian worship and how it relates to the Hindu concept of *yajna*, or sacrifice, has been much discussed by Indian theologians. I cannot enter this debate here but want to refer to the discussion which arose in the Ashram Aikya newsletter as a result of a letter written by Fr. Bede Griffiths on the place of Eucharistic worship in the ashram. For him, it appeared, the sacred place of the ashram was more associated with meditation and yoga than with the Eucharisitic prayer of the church.

This discussion does have a bearing on another question which has been thought about in the context of the Indian church. What is the place of baptism in the understanding of sacred space? Theologian Aloysius Pieris has suggested that the Christian church has itself to be baptised in the waters of Indian spirituality and that baptism should be understood not only in terms of baptism of individuals but of cultures. Baptism as diksha, or the final initiation into the mystery of Christ's death and resurrection, does need to be understood in the Christian context of India. It has been very much misunderstood by Hindus who have simply seen it as a way of creating disjunction between Hindu and Christian culture.

The significance of water and the ritual of bathing has been essential to the Hindu concept of sacred space. It has been understood as the culmination of a spiritual journey, not just as the sign of having a new social identity. To finally pass through the waters and go to the further shore is the ultimate meaning of the Hindu spiritual quest, or *sadhana*. It comes at the end, not the beginning, of the pilgrimage.

Sr. Sara Grant, commenting on her own experiences as the *acharya* of the Christa Prema Seva Ashram in Pune, has discussed how pilgrim Hindus who came to the Christian ashram wanted to share in the Eucharist as the *puja* of the ashram. For them, as they expressed it, part of the welcome which the ashram had to offer was to be able to experience the guru of the ashram, whom they understood as present in the Eucharistic elements of bread and wine. This caused problems as the Eucharist is denied to those who have not first been baptised. Sr. Sara Grant did suggest that the Eucharist could be understood as an invitation, in the same way that Jesus said to his disciples that they had been drawn to follow him because of the miracle which he had performed when multiplying the loaves and fishes. In the Sikh tradition the shared meal is the celebration of a common purpose of coming together.

There is certainly some ambiguity in equating the Christian understanding of Eucharist with the *garbha griha*. Fr. Michael Amalados questioned whether *arathi* should be performed when the holy elements are lifted up with the priestly prayer "In him, through him, and with him..." which is the prayer of Jesus offering himself to God. The purpose of *arathi*, which is to reveal the presence, is not intended here.

What is needed in this discussion on the place of Indian forms of architecture, and symbolism in the context of Christian acts of worship is to understand what we mean by the presence of Christ in the midst of his believers. "When two or three are gathered together, I am there in your midst" Jesus told his followers. Do the sacred mysteries present Jesus or represent him? This was one of the points raised during a discussion on the purpose of Christian art in India held at a workshop on the theology of art organised by the Gurukul Lutheran Research Centre in Madras, May 1978. For many, the purpose of using art forms within the context of the church is only meaningful as a vehicle for communicating the gospel. In other words, the culture provides a language, or idiom, in which to present the message found in the gospel. Incarnation however concerns more than that. Christ himself is made present within a culture.

What we are searching for is a centre which will give a focus to a faith experience. A model for the home, which could perhaps give another way of understanding a culture, is to take the typical house with a courtyard. This house, which has an inner space, is as much to be found in the Middle East as in north-east Asia. The courtyard is at the heart of the home but it is also open to the skies. It has a small garden where plants are grown. In many Hindu villages, the centre courtyard of the home contains the holy *tulsi* plant (the basil shrub) which represents healing and has a sweet aroma. Here is an image of nature at the heart of the home. Water is also often represented in the form of a small pool, as found in many Muslim homes where a source of water, either in a container like a pool or as a spring or fountain, provides a sacred source of life within the household.

In the image of the enclosed garden many traditions come together and ritual is minimised. One of the basic tendencies which characterises all efforts at internalising spiritual life is to go beyond mere outward forms, including rituals, to find an inner meaning. In the future, church life - especially in a culture like that of India - should be much more a part of daily family life and not so bound down to the institutional expression of a highly organised ecclesiology based on an understanding of the church dominated by priests and professional religious. The church of the future will be, not only a church which is inserted into many different cultures, but also a church which enters into the lives of ordinary people, giving new meaning to the sanctity of the home.

Lectern in the Ashirvad chapel.

8

The Church as a Seat of Power

While the prayer room is a very intimate space, the church as a public building is not only the extension of the inner world of the individual worshipper but also represents the power of the whole believing community. The church expresses the worshippers' sense of belonging to a wider pattern of community relationships which include both the economic and political dimensions of human life. Those who want to separate the public from the private and the secular from the religious, forget that these opposites are interwoven like the warp and woof of a garment. It is in this context that we have also to view the moment of spiritual conversion - is it something purely personal, and therefore private, or does it in fact constitute a public statement, involving the self-perception of a whole community and, as a result, inevitably affecting the way in which society is constituted?

The cathedral represents the very limit of a Christian presence understood as a public expression of faith. It is the religious equivalent of what in the whole polity stands for the state. The cathedral as a built form demonstrates the most visible and hierarchical manifestation of religious power, as it addresses itself to the corporate identity which constitutes the nation. There has always been a tense relationship between the religious institution and the political armature of the state. We find in the building of the church the dialectics of such opposing stresses. On one hand is the demand for an inner spirituality but on the other hand, faith is articulated through symbols of group identity and influence. The building can be analysed as a statement concerning the power which a particular community exercises on the whole social fabric, especially in a pluralistic society like India, where many faith systems interact.

In the so called "conversion movements", through which large groups of individuals decide to change publicly from one religious identity to another, we find interests at work which are not simply personal. In discussing the whole phenomenon of conversion as a cultural process rather than an individual option, Fr. Aloysius Pieris suggests that what we are calling a "conversion movement" is a paradigmatic shift from a cosmic world-view to a metacosmic one.

How this shift expresses itself in the choice of architectural forms would be a fascinating study in itself. In this chapter we can only hint at some of the options which have been taken through specific examples. The changes involved relate not only to traditional images but to the whole question of modernity as opposed to tradition, urbanisation as a new culture of a market economy and what this means in terms of an individual's social status. In a society like that of traditional India, where the group acts in tandem with individualistic patterns of belief, the will of the whole community has a relationship to the personal intentions of each of its members in a way that has now been lost in the west. In a traditional tribe, as also in a village where family links are still very strong, the individual person belongs to a corporate identity which generates a form of consciousness quite different from the mind-set concerned with ethical choices which prevail in a depersonalised urban context.

The tension in India between gospel and culture is also the tension between the demands of an inner private pilgrimage and group pressures coming from caste or lineage. The moment of conversion tends to confound the private with the public and the individual seeker with a sense of loyalty to a wider social entity. It is precisely here that a cultural disjunction often takes place, whereby the new convert loses all cultural moorings and becomes completely disoriented in a world of competing cultural claims.

During the 1930's there were a number of conversion movements which greatly affected the relationship of the church to the nationalist movement. Ramsay MacDonald, who was then Prime Minister of England, made important changes in electoral procedures, allowing for separate electorates for different communities. This led to Christian as well as Muslim electoral groupings. Then there was the demand for a separate electorate for the Dalits, who felt that in a caste-ridden society such as India they would not be given a fair chance unless their electoral rights were protected. Mahatma Gandhi opposed this idea as he felt that it would lead eventually to the splitting up of the nation so he began his famous fast-to-death in 1932 at Pune, where he was at the time imprisoned. This resulted in the Dalits abandoning their demands.

In 1935 Dr. Ambedkar made an important declaration at the Yeola conference, when he advised Dalits to officially leave Hinduism, as they would never receive justice within the framework of the caste system. He further suggested that Dalits should opt for some other religion: for example, either Christianity or Islam. The fact that Christians had been awarded at that time a separate electorate meant that by joining Christianity the Dalits would be able to establish a political base outside the Hindu fold. It was this kind of political manouevering that gave rise to what came to be called the "conversion movements" and lead to large numbers of Dalits joining various denominations of the church.

Gandhi, as well as Rajagopalachariar in the south of India, were extremely upset about these conversion movements. They were anxious that should these movements escalate, the Christian vote would make a sizeable impression on the larger Hindu polity, even though Christians were still a small minority in comparison with other religious groups such as the Muslim community. An important figure in the debate concerning conversion was Bishop Azariah, who himself, came from a Dalit background and whose bishopric was unusual in that it was very much village-based. He was a remarkable man in many ways, with a strong sense of mission. He made a significant contribution to the first World Missionary Conference in Edinburgh, 1910, where he was one of the few young non-Europeans present and read a paper on "Co-operation between foreign and native workers in the younger churches". In 1939 he completed the construction of a cathedral in Dornakal, Andhra Pradesh, which was dedicated on the feast of the Epiphany. Nine bishops participated in its consecration and there were nearly 2000 communicants. Just 35 years earlier there had been only seven Christians in that whole district

For Bishop Azariah, the building of the cathedral was a visual manifestation of his whole understanding of mission, especially mission to the Dalits. Perhaps it would not be too fanciful to suggest that the way in which he built the cathedral, "converted" religious symbols of Hindu origin as well as Muslim architectural forms. The very building has something to say about his understanding of conversion as a process in itself. He argued that to be converted does not mean losing one's Indian identity. He saw himself as an ardent patriot but he did not think that Indian identity meant Hindu identity. He was not afraid of using elements from the past but he wanted something to emerge which would be a new synthesis. He felt free to borrow from Muslim local traditions since the state of Hyderabad, and also the earlier Sultanate of Bijapur were not far away, and to mix what was earlier known as "saracenic" with Hindu motifs. He wrote with passion:

"Christianity has always stood for conversion, and for changing people from one society to another. 'If any man is in Christ he is a new creature' and a new creature can only thrive in a new environment...

Dornakal Cathedral - Church of South India.

"Would India's freedom mean a return to the old caste tyranny? From recent experiences (the Indian Christian) is not at all sure it will not. The educated Christian in an academic sort of way desires complete freedom: but would the rural Christian be free when India's freedom comes ?....
"Nationalism is apt to be identified with loyalty to the ancient religion of the land and this identification might easily look with suspicion and disfavour on any religion which is not supposed to belong to the soil."
(Susan Billington Harper "The Politics of Conversion" *Indo-British Review*, pp 147-175)

In statements such as these Bishop Azariah opposed Gandhi and other leaders who felt that such mass conversions were not coming from a religious motivation but rather a political one and that, unless Dalits stayed within Hinduism and reformed it from within, their status would never change but become institutionalised in the form of another social identity. Even Dr. Ambedkar questioned Bishop Azariah about the ultimate status of Dalit Christians within the Church. He claimed that caste divisions had already entered the Christian church and by joining the Church, Dalits would simply become "Dalit Christians".

In Kerala, for example, the Syrian Christians believed very strongly that they came from a high caste background. Certainly, the Syrian Christians have struggled to maintain a position in society which is on the same level as other high caste members of society. Syrian Christians have, in fact, practiced caste restrictions, refusing to admit into their homes those who are Dalits in their part of the country. Dalits who became Christian in Kerala joined either the Latin Church or, later, various Protestant missions.

Another example of the mixture of styles is St Mary's Votive Church in Kilpauk, Madras. On December 8, 1942, Fr Michael Murray made a promise that if Madras escaped destructiuon by the Japanese a votive church would be built in

St Mary's honour. A Frenchman donated the funds and property and F.R. Davis architect of the Catholic Centre in Madras and the shrine at Perambur designed the church which was consecrated April 1952 (see page 157).

When Laurie Baker was commissioned, soon after the Vatican Council, to design a cathedral for the Syro-Malankara Church in Tiruvalla, the cathedral expressed the new-found identity of the Syrian Orthodox Church, now in communion with Rome but very conscious of its past. Here was a grand opportunity for Laurie Baker to experiment with the conical roof structures which he so admired in the Hindu temples of Kerala. But actually the whole atmosphere in this cathedral is quite different from anything you will ever find in a Hindu temple.

In a letter which Laurie Baker wrote to me December 1987 when he was working on the Tiruvalla Cathedral, he described an impression of Westminster Cathedral which he had visited as a child of five years when his father took him to see the building then being constructed in 1922:.

"It was just bare bricks and concrete awaiting (though at that age I didn't know it) to be covered all over with mosaic and marble and gold leaf etc. It was a bright sunny Sunday morning and the sun streamed in through temporary plain glass windows stabbing the blue incense laden air inside with long parallel strings of light - until they lit some Bishop or Cardinal in vivid red and gold high up above me in the great stage. Again, although I of course knew nothing of such things then, the sheer scale brought about by these bare bricks and gaily clothed people was just so overwhelming I couldn't hold back tears, which naturally my mother took to be tears of torture-cum-boredom of a 5 year old forced to sit through a service in Latin, understanding nothing and probably hungry and thirsty."

This same sense of vast spaces which give an almost cosmic

setting for ritual, which Laurie Baker managed to create in his Tiruvalla Cathedral (below).

Tiruvalla Cathedral

(above) Soaring conical roof using typical Kerala woodwork.

(right) Entrance to Turivalla Cathedral compound.

Photos: Caroline Mackenzie

The concept of the cathedral in Christian tradition is linked closely to the city as it evolved in the west. The Bible seems to span two powerful images. One in Genesis where we read of the enclosed garden of creation and the other in the book of Revelation, where we are confronted with the vision of a new Jerusalem, a "city in which there is no temple" because the city itself is the throne of God. The word "cathedral" derives from the Greek word for seat, indicating its function as the place where the throne of the bishop is positioned.

Dornakal Cathedral is very unusual in that it was intended by Bishop Azariah as a cathedral for village India. But the fact remains that the majority of Indian Christians live in cities, particularly the cities which were created by the colonialists. Those living in rural areas who are converted to Christianity, particularly the Dalits and Adivasis, often want to shift to cities after they become Christian. So the process of being converted to Christianity is already a step in the direction of urbanisation.

Dr. Abraham Ayrookuzhiel considers this natural. He pointed out that it is in the city that the kind of marginalisation which Dalit or Adivasi face in conservative rural India begins to crumble. In the villages of India, the so-called depressed classes can never find the environment which enables them to become the new persons about whom Bishop Azariah speaks.

Not all Indian cities are modern. Perhaps one of the oldest cities in the world, even predating a city like Rome, is Varanasi on the river Ganges. This city has been a holy city by a holy river and, in many ways, one could relate this ancient centre of learning and Indian culture to the vision of the eschatological city which we find in the Bible. But this is by no means a new city. Rather, it is a very ancient one, built over layers and layers of human settlements going back to neolithic times.

From prehistoric times, on a bend of the Ganges where, for the last time, the holy river is believed to look back to its source in the Himalayas to the north, a ford across the river enabled travellers from the East to cross to the western limits of the *doab* a plain between the two river systems. Because all roads leading from the east to the west of the Indian peninsula had to pass this way, Varanasi became a centre for both pilgrims and traders. It is the place where many cultures have had their centre. Jains as well as Buddhists congregated here. The King of Varanasi had given to the Lord Buddha a garden in Sarnath where he preached his first sermon. Varanasi, or Kashi as it was known to the Hindus, later became a centre for Shaivism in the north, attracting many Hindu divines from the south. Finally, the Muslims took it over, destroying several times the Viswanath Temple and building on its ruins a great mosque which is still resented by Hindus. Some Hindus want to reclaim the site in order to re-build a temple dedicated to the Lord of the Universe which was, in ancient times, one of the principal temples of the north. About forty percent of the present population of this Hindu holy city is now Muslim. They are mainly weavers who have always been seen as outcaste (Nita Kumar "The Artisans of Banaras" Orient Longman 1995).

There are no more than three to four thousand Christians in Varanasi, most of them located in the Cantonment area which was added to the city by the British to establish the army and the workers on the railways. Varanasi was, and continues to be, an important junction. Because of its religious importance as the heart of Indian religious history, the Indian Missionary Society arrived in Varanasi to set up the headquarters of one of the first indigenous orders dedicated to the spread of Christianity in the north. A prefecture for the Varanasi/Gorakhpur area came into effect in 1946 and the prefect took up residence in the city. The well-known Franciscan, Rt Rev Malenfant, was then the prefect apostolic. It was only in 1970 that Varanasi was finally made into a diocese, with Fr. Patrick D'Souza as its first Bishop.

The Missionary Sisters of the Queen of the Apostles was founded in Germany by a charismatic priest, Fr. Bodewig who was, for a few years, a missionary in north India. He attempted to establish an ashram-type of life, on the lines of De Nobili at

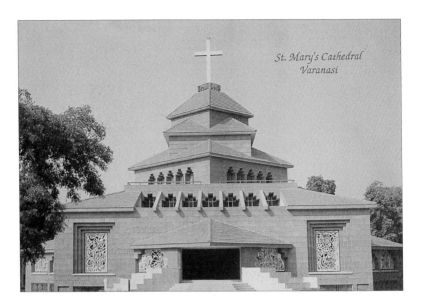

St Mary's Cathedral Varanasi (Benares)

(left) Window grill based on the vision of the woman in Revelation.

Egatpuri, as early as the mid-1870's. Subsequently, he returned to Germany and became a priest in the Cologne diocese. In 1911 he wrote to the Bishop of Allahabad:"Many years ago after mature deliberation I have bound myself by a vow to do whatever I can in order to raise in Varanasi a worthy temple to the Immaculate Conception..." It was because of this link that the Cologne diocese supported the project of building a cathedral in Varanasi.

Varanasi has attracted missionary zeal among foreign missionaries and also Indian Christians. There is a deep connection, going back to biblical times, between a sense of mission and the dream of an eschatological city. The Holy City of Varanasi has become a focus for the missionary efforts of the church because of its symbolic importance in India. Asked why such a large and imposing cathedral was planned for this city when there are so few Christians actually living in Varanasi, the Bishop said that it was intended as a sign for the future of the presence of the Indian Church.

Further, by gathering here those village Christians scattered over the vast Gangetic plain, the Bishop hoped that they would feel a greater sense of their importance within a much wider church which spreads all over the world. The Cathedral is planned with two storeys, the bottom level being completely taken up with an exhibition using puppets, and elaborate scenes made from papier mache, showing the biblical story. This is intended as a way of introducing scenes from the Christian scriptures to pilgrims from the countryside who come to visit Varanasi, in the same way that the events of the Ramayana have been presented for popular devotion in the famous *Tulsimanasa Mandir* at the centre of the town.

When Fr. Patrick D'Souza decided to build a new cathedral for his diocese, he commissioned architect Krishna Menon to present designs which had an Indian character. Krishna Menon, listing what he considered to be the possible ingredients for such a design, came up with the following points:
- A multi-faceted plan form to be generated through the

development of simple geometric elements.
- Sloping, tiled roofs which become necessary in India's climate.
- The expressive use of the *jali* to demarcate the inside and outside.
- The practice of circumambulation around venerated objects.
- The use of the corbelling to span distance.

When I was asked to be involved in the planning process my contribution was to suggest the structure of the mandala which I had been working on as a basis for Indian Christian iconography since my first series of Christian mandalas painted in 1967. I also proposed to design a series of *Jali* designs for the 21 spaces for *Jali* work that went round the enclosing walls of the built area. Jali literally means "net" and is applied to perforated stone or brick walls designed for decoration or ventilation These designs are meant to be seen from the outside of the building and attempt to bring out the connection between the life of Christ and his journey from the waters of baptism to his final passion in the holy city of Jerusalem.

By understanding the cathedral as a mandala, rather than the favoured basilican plan of the west, the problem was where to locate the presidium. The mandala, which is a central symbol of sacred space in the Hindu/ Buddhist tradition, depicts the cosmos in which the divine power of the deity emanates from within creation. Christian and Muslim architecture, on the other hand, has tended to represent the transcendance of God beyond the cosmos of creation, the worshipper being invited to look beyond the built forms of Church or Mosque towards a God whose throne is beyond our world.

While working on this project between the years 1988-93 the architect, Krishna Menon, drew my attention to an interesting church built in Delhi. This was the St. Thomas Church (see page 154), built between 1971-73 by architect Oscar Pereira, who has since settled in America. The church uses the massed structure so characteristic of the Delhi sultanate, deriving from the kind of Indian Islamic architecture which probably first emerged in Bijapur and which subsequently influenced the Moghul buildings of the north. Here, a kind of tumulus effect is created by the piling up of solid masonry in geometric patterns elaborating on a simple ground plan often octagonal in design. This can be seen in many tombs scattered around the old Muslim town of Mehrauli where the famous mosque of Qutb was constructed out of the broken parts of ancient Hindu and Jain temples in that area.

I believe this Church had influenced Krishna Menon, who combined various elements, including Syrian Christian patterning of roof structures, to create a kind of architecture formed by the piling up of built members. Earlier, Lutyens, the architect of New Delhi, advised his collaborator and friend, Herbert Baker to

> "build a vasty mess (sic) of rough concrete, elephant-wise on a very simple rectangular-cum-octagon plan, dome in space anyhow, cut off square. Overlay with a veneer of stone patterns like laying a vertical tile floor..." (R.G. Irving "Indian Summer" p.43, Pub Delhi 1981)

Hindu architecture, according to Lutyens, merely aped wooden construction in stone, while Mughal building though of a higher order, consisted of "masses of brick and concrete covered with decoration". *Jalis* he acknowledged as "perfectly beautiful".

Buildings are impressive either in terms of their height or their weight and solidity. The public building as a monument is a visual symbol of how power functions in society, either through images of gravity, or as a series of steps leading up to heaven. Both the cathedral at Varanasi and the earlier building at Dornakal, have tended to use Islamic prototypes combined with Hindu detailing to give a sense of cosmic symbolism and transcendent power.

These principles of Indian architecture can be traced back to stupa forms such as those at Sarnath, In them, the sacred

The church of St Thomas in Rama Krishna Puram, Delhi shows the influence of Moghul tomb structures.

building is understood as a massive constructed mountain, the walls of which have an almost fortress-like solidity.

Holy ground has been associated with two ancient prototypes. On the one side there is the primordial grove which has been pictured as a natural paradise from which the human race originated. At the other extreme is the city, with its fortified walls, resisting both the erosions of natural changes brought about by elemental forces as well as attacks from enemy peoples. From pre-historic times the temple has represented a strongly-guarded treasure whose enclosing walls are intended to keep out intruders. As noted earlier, the sacred place is a public monument, often situated at the very centre of the metropolitan city complex. The city temple and the metropolitan cathedral symbolise the seat of power from which secular as well as sacred authority derives its force.

There is a constant ambiguity in church history between the image of a divine institution representing those who are redeemed from oppression, the poor and rejected, and a church presence which is a powerful force in itself. The cathedral, even when it draws together a scattered and rural community, stands out against the other powerful structures which have represented the agents of oppression. Without taking into account this balancing of powers within society and the way in which power is expressed through buildings, the symbolic function of architectural forms cannot be understood. It is in this context also that we have to review the whole debate on cost. When Laurie Baker designed Tiruvalla Cathedral he wanted to demonstrate that his ideas about low-cost building could be extended to such a public edifice as a cathedral. He wanted to show that an impressive monument to a community's identity need not cost too much.

The influential modern Indian architect, Charles Correa has thought a great deal about the city landscape and the requirements of a new urbanised architecture. In his famous church in Bombay, the Salvacao Church, Bandra, built 1974-77, the architect draws on the ancient city planning of Mohenjo daro, by using a modular structure to build up an urbanised space of inter-connected private and public areas. This pattern of using open and enclosed spaces within an overall grid format influenced the structure he proposed for the Gandhi exhibition hall at the Gandhi ashram in Ahmedabad. This structure also influenced the design of Snehasadan, an Indian Christian dialogue centre which Fr. Mathew Lederle helped develop in Pune with the help of one of the followers of Charles Correa.

The church space which Correa designed at Bandra is conceived as a series of interlocking courtyards and covered spaces. The emphasis is not on height, as in the western church, but on the horizontal networking of liturgical spaces, taking design elements from monolithic structures which are to be found in India in temple architecture. He rejects the use of decorative detailing or borrowing from any superficial rendering of traditional native styles. Rather, he aims at creating primordial and primitive forms, drawing from the ideas of Le Corbusier in his chapel at Ronchamp.

Laurie Baker, discussing the question of cost when building a church, insists on the use of simple and natural materials. In this he has been influenced by what I described elsewhere as ashram architecture. Charles Correa, by using extensively modern materials like reinforced concrete and glass, has been accused of adding to the cost of his buildings. Modern architecture is associated with a new way of using material resources which were not earlier available to the builder, having only recently been developed through modern technologies. The modern city, itself a product of the modern scientific and technological age, uses pre-fabricated materials which tend to separate the urban world from its natural surroundings and contribute to our present ecological crisis.

Here we face the same dilemma which was discussed in relation to the ashram. There we found an effort to return to basics and to create an architecture without decorative frills. But what was thought to be primal and elemental in that setting is different from the "primitive" forms which Charles Correa tries to create with his truncated cones in prefabricated concrete. What is lost is a sense of rootedness in the earth and the quality of simple natural materials. It is a problem similar to that faced by modern cities. The city represents a loss of relationship with the elemental in terms of ordinary natural forms. The city celebrates the artificial.

St Mary's Votive Church, Kilpauk. Madras (above and opposite)
Built following the 1939-45 war as a gesture of thanks
that the Japanese armies did not invade India.

The chapel at Muttattur in Villupuram Dist, South Arcot.

The chapel is built on a plinth with minaret towers at each corner.

The Mandapam structure (left) is at the front.

9

Tribal and Dalit Churches

Over the last ten to fifteen years there has been a great deal of discussion on what constitutes Dalit or Adivasi cultures in India. The basic argument is that these cultures are quite distinct from mainline Hindu or Buddhist traditions which have emerged out of the philosophic reflections which we find in the Vedanta, or the "end of the Vedas".

The church in India has contact with more than a hundred different tribal groups. Each has its own distinct culture and different tribes in India are found to come from differing racial backgrounds. However, it has been suggested that there does constitute something which we can call tribal culture which can be distinguished from the culture that developed as a result of the process known as civilisation. There are people who claim that tribal cultures have a civilisation of their own but here we are assuming that tribal cultures constitute mainly nomadic or primitive agricultural communities which have not developed a highly sophisticated technology of their own. Although we do find the emergence of certain technologies like iron smelting, the city as the centre of a settled agrarian economy is foreign to such communities.

The culture of the tribal or Adivasi people also remains at the preliterate, or oral level, and this affects the images they use, because images are already on the way towards literacy, as we see in the development of certain ancient scripts from pictographs. Stories, particularly creation stories which recount the origins of the tribe are also histories in a primal sense and are the main vehicles for cultural identity. The creation stories are also different in character from the myths which we find in the Sanskritic traditions - for example, the Hindu or Jain traditions. These myths *(Puranas)* are first of all written down and have gone through a long process of literary refinement. They may have originated from earlier creation stories but they have been worked over by a highly sophisticated literary tradition. Further, these stories are generally concerned with the creating of a cosmology dominated by gods and goddesses. In contrast, Adivasi stories, though mentioning various creator spirits or beings, are mainly concerned with recounting the origins of the tribe. The Sanskritic tradition of the Brahmanic synthesis, for example, has a whole world of inter-related myths presenting a vast pantheon of extra-terrestrial beings. The Adivasi community generally has one major creation story and a network of legends and folk tales about animals ghosts etc. which shade off into being proverbs or parables presenting anecdotal meanings which help to give foundation to what might be called tribal values.

Dr Ram Dayal Munda, the former Vice Chancellor of Ranchi University, has stressed these tribal values, which he claims are very different from the values of the so-called "civilised" peoples who look towards the city and its culture as a model. The Adivasis, for example, do not feel that storing or competing are values, nor have they created a hierarchy which is basic to the later city cultures. Adivasi communities are in general more egalitarian, having a social structure which is called by some oligarchic, or even republican. Actually, Buddhist culture has been closer to this adivasi value system than to Hindu Brahmanaical culture which supported the caste system. There are many who feel that the ideal of the monk or wandering *sanyasi*, who leaves the city for the forests, rejecting caste hierarchies, has much in common with the tribal hero, or *shaman*. Mircea Eliade argues in his great work on yoga and transformation that ideas which underlie yogic doctrines go back to ancient shamanistic practices found among pre-literate tribal communities before the advent of settled agriculture. (Willard R Trask "Yoga: Immortality and Freedom", pub Routledge, Keegan Paul 1954).

The process of Christianising Adivasi communities is in many ways also a process of urbanising them. The pressures of expanding civilisation on the environment have made it increasingly difficult to maintain the life-style which characterised ancient Adivasi communities. This process has been a slow continual tendency, which recent changes in technology and the globalisation of the economy have merely accelerated. In other words, conversion to Christianity has gone hand in hand with modernisation. As forests were cut down and changed over to plantations and the cultivation of crops with seasonal ploughing took place, tribal or Adivasi communities found they could no longer continue in their natural habitat and felt they have to find some point of entry into the world of modern India. The ancient caste system which grew up out of the hierarchical society which characterised city-based Hindu dynasties leaves little room for the accommodation of primal peoples. They therefore felt drawn to become either Muslims or Christians.

Another complication has been the social position of Dalits, otherwise known as outcastes. Dalit culture is not the same as Adivasi cultures. The Dalits have passed through a long historical process by which their craft-based skills have been appropriated and accommodated into the urbanised societies of the dominant castes. These ancient craft communities have served as menials, but also as basic technicians who have served a vital role in the building up of an urban-rural complex of villages subservient to city states. The Dalits have often been treated as slaves by the cultured and lettered elite. Crafts people like weavers, potters, metal workers, especially blacksmiths and leather workers who are associated with butchers and scavengers have all been placed within the outcaste category of Hindu society. These Dalits may have come originally from ancient tribal groups but they are even looked down upon by

Adivasis who also regard craft workers as belonging to a lower order, their work being somehow associated with ritual pollution. The Dalits, as early technicians, were absorbed and domesticated by the prevailing hierarchical caste-based society, assuming the lowest place in the social system. On the other hand, some tribal communities have in the past been absorbed into the caste system as warrior clans *(kshatriyas)* and even *brahmins* (priests). The outcaste, which includes both Dalits and Adivasi peoples, represent conquered and generally rejected people who have been either marginalised like some Adivasis who have remained in the forests or used as grist for the agricultural mill as cheap labour. In the process of being uprooted and scattered sometimes whole communities and their way of life has been decimated. It is considered that twenty to twenty-five percent of the Indian population fall within this outcaste category, of which half may be Dalits and the remaining half Adivasis.

In recent times there has been growing literature on this subject. The present thrust in theological reflection in India has been concerned with the place of Adivasi and Dalit cultures in the church today. Various theologates have been talking about Dalit and Adivasi theology. In the Old Testament we have a pattern very similar to the process which we are observing in India. The Hebrew people seem to have emerged from an ancient Middle East confederacy of tribes. At some point in time these tribes became indebted to, and enslaved by, the emerging civilisation of Egypt. Later they suffered a period of enslavement by Babylonian and Assyrian civilisations. The Exodus story and the later admonitions of the prophets, related to a process of liberation whereby a subjugated people rediscovered their native freedom and dignity. Later, these wandering tribes proceeded to settle down and developed a civilisation with their own king and holy city at Jerusalem. It was at this point they built a temple, which in many ways reflected the temples which were emerging in the surrounding civilisations. The temple as a structure is closely associated with the symbolic meaning of the city.

In India, the rise of temple cities, as for example at Mathura or Varanasi in the north and Tanjore or Madurai in the south, became the focus for a hierarchical and caste-structured society which the temple complex reflected. Access is given to the temple at various levels, depending on the level of society to which you belong. Outcastes are not allowed into the temple. Even the temple festival, when the deity is put into a decorated chariot *(ratha)* and carried or pushed out of the temple to make a ritualist tour of the surrounding city, is an occasion when caste divisions are further consolidated.

When communities who have been classified by Hindu society as outcaste opt to become Christian or Muslim in order to find a new position within the community the new converts want access to the sacred which will give them a new status in society. There are two ways of doing this. One way is to go back to the past and find cultural roots there. Another is to build a church bearing no resemblance to the temple structure The western model of a church offered a clear alternative to the temple and was often situated at the centre of the new cities which the colonialists built. The church gave its members a new identity, especially to those Indian Christians who as Dalits had formerly been denied access to the Hindu temple.

However, this identity presented problems when the colonial empires crumbled or changed their way of operating. Indian Christians were then seen as the remnant of a foreign rule, which ultimately meant they were marginalised from mainstream Indian society. Those who became Christian as Dalits were often simply seen as Dalit Christians and their former position in society remained unchanged. This is partly due to discrimination practised in the church itself where caste differences continue to be remembered and even maintained. The present position of Christian Dalits as twice-alienated is often a direct outcome of nationalism and a return to a Hindu caste-ridden society which has become politicised. In this climate the tendency of urbanised Christians is to take on a new role as part of a global culture which has brought with it a global economy. Indian Christians want to identify with a way of life that extends beyond national frontiers and they resent attempts to put the individual back into a traditional Hindu cultural mould. It is in this situation that we find a number of earlier attempts at making churches in an Indian style are rejected by Dalit as well as Adivasi Christians.

In this context, Indian Christians have felt the need to affirm a new identity as strongly as possible. But is this identity to be confused with a Hindu culture? Increasingly, Dalits and Adivasis have stressed the fact that they have never been accepted as Hindus: that is, as part of the Hindu social system, and so dissociate themselves from Hinduism as a whole. So now, after experimenting with the idea of becoming a new type of Hindu albeit a "Hindu Christian", many Indian Christians feel it is important to insist that they are not Hindus. This obviously affects the buildings in which they would like to worship and the rites of worship with which they feel most comfortable.

Recently a number of churches have been constructed to serve the particular needs of Christian Adivasis or Dalits. One example is a group of churches in Gujarat, which came about through the missionary work of Jesuits in that area. The tribals of Zankhva, Gujarat, can truly call the Isunath Mandir "their church". In truth, the church has been built by them and for them and is of their culture. Once the need for a church was felt, the idea was discussed with the elders of the locality, the Catechists, the Sisters and Fathers. A rough sketch was proposed to Fr. Carsi who finally prepared a very simple, but beautiful plan.

> "The selection of the artisans was made after a competition held at Zankhvav for adivasi wood-carvers and painters. The creativity of our aboriginals is clearly seen here, as we have made use of their aesthetic sense ; their culture is truly the inspiration behind the Church" (Fr Galdos "A New Church in a Tribal Area", p. 338, Vidyajyoti, 1980).

Jesus is seen as an aboriginal, that is a vasavo, a first settler. The well-known Indian artist Frank Wesley once explained why he painted Jesus looking like an aboriginal tribal person. He said: "Jesus said 'Before Abraham was, I am.' Therefore he saw himself as an Aboriginal person".

The Aboriginal people called vasavo cleared the jungle and built their village. In this process they became simple agriculturalists. Fr. Galdos gave a theological meaning to this process of being a settler:

> "The Church, more than a shrine, is the House of the Lord Jesus. He is our first "Vasavo", who had to leave the House of his Father to settle down (Jn 1.14) in the forest of sin, and create a new house for us, a new Church, where we all live as brothers." (Fr Galdos op cit p.338)

The characteristic form of a tribal settlement in a large common house is imitated in the form of the church. The entrance to the church is on the broad side of the rectangular hall, this being understood as the welcoming side which is wide open to visitors and has a verandah or porch along one side, the south side of the building. The tower which is placed on the roof of this ancestral home is a place for ancestral spirits to dwell.

Tribal faith systems give great importance to the ancestral spirits which are housed in vessel-like containers or in stones which are used as boundary markers. The various spirits of the Christian villages are made present in such stones which are grouped around the base of the cross in the church. In this way, the wandering souls of the dead are given a home or place to rest. The tabernacle is also given an important place in the church as an ark, like the Jewish ark of the covenant, which is based on two deer-shaped pillars.

The wooden pillars of the church and the great doors of the church are richly carved with tribal symbols and scenes of the tribal life of the *vasavos*.

A similar effort at inculturation has been attempted among the Naga tribes of Nagaland, North-East India, where the traditional *morung*, or chieftain's house, has been adapted as a basis for church architecture. The *morung* is characterised by great horn-like projections on the roof, which indicate the feast which the chief has given to the whole community. An attempt has been made to model the new Roman Catholic Cathedral at Kohima on this pattern.

Among the Dalits, the problem of finding an architectural prototype is more complex. The Dalit has no particular or distinctive form of architecture. The temple is, therefore, appropriated. An example of this is the Shrine of Unteshwari, the Mother of the Camels and, by extension, the camel drivers in Budasan village near the town of Kadi in Gujarat. A number of the converts to Christianity in this area came from the *raval* caste who are traditional camel drivers.

A decision was taken in 1969 to convert an extensive property belonging to the Church (107 acres) into a pilgrimage centre for the surrounding converts of central and north Gujarat. As Fr. M. Diaz Garriz explains, the enthusiasm for pilgrimage is widespread in this area, especially at the time of the ancient agricultural festival of *Navrathri*, or nine nights, in the autumn when the mother goddess is worshipped by Hindus.

"Our leaders felt that since everybody around was in those days celebrating a festival with great eclat, it was bad for the new converts to feel culturally cut off from their caste brothers, and therefore the right thing for us was to celebrate during the same days a festival in honour of the Mother of Jesus. Therefore the first annual pilgrimage-cum melo (fair) on the chosen date of Atham sud Aso (Ashwini) was held in 1970." (Diaz Garriz "The Shrine of Unteshwari Mata - A Step in Inculturation." p 13. 1980)

There is a strong element of folk culture to be found in this shrine, with a very solid figure of Mary and the Child with a

(above)
The Uteshwari pilgrimage centre in Gujarat.

(left)
Carved figure of St Francis Xavier like an Indian Guru holding a palm leaf manuscript.
Interior of Uteshwari.

Photos: Sanjay.

(above)
Mosaic by Shanti Shah in Uteshwari showing the flight into Egypt with Mary seated on a camel. Photo: Sanjay

(below)
Mosaic dome with mirrors tells the Magnificat story.
Built by craftsmen of Madhya Pradesh.

camel mosaic in the background. In fact the dome of the central hall, which has the characteristic form of the typical *solanki* temple of Gujarat, is often dedicated to *ras lila,* or the dance of creation. Here in the Unteshwari shrine is a lively ceiling mosaic with mirror work representing the Magnificat, depicting dancing figures reminiscent of folk dancing known as *gharbha,* which is very popular during the Narvrathri season.

The inter-faith prayer house designed for Maithri Ashram at Sunanda village in Kolar district was a new experiment in ashram life initiated by the dynamic Sr. Celestine and also Fr. Claude D'Souza. The local community for whom the ashram was established were originally bonded labourers who had been brought to the vicinity of the Kolar goldfields by the British under the indentured labour system which, in fact, was a type of slavery. A system of indebtedness bound these workers to continue their life of hard labour for very little reward, unable to gain freedom because of the bond under which they had been originally contracted often many generations earlier. A recent decision of the Indian Government has freed all bonded labourers from their indebtedness.

Despite the cancellation of all past debts, local daily wage earners remain vulnerable to a whole system of village credit through which moneyed landlords, who act as money lenders, exact heavy interest and in lieu of payment demand free labour from those who fall into the debt trap.

The ashram was established to help such bonded labourers, through conscientisation and mutual forms of aid, to find their own freedom .

Those whom the ashram serves are mostly not Christian and the vast majority are Dalits. Services are held with *bhajans* or devotional songs and sometimes plays are performed. These small plays are intended to make the people aware of their situation and history. There is also a place set aside for the reservation of the blessed sacrament, where those who wish can go to pray and be quiet for a time in meditation.

Miss Caroline MacKenzie prepared a series of symbolic designs and grills to enclose this sacred space, representing

Tabernacle setting in the meditation room of Maitri Sagar Ashram, Kolar Gold Fields, Karnataka.
Setting and photo: Caroline Mackenzie.

Tabernacle Setting in the meditation room of
Aikya Alayam Ashram, Madras.
Photo: Caroline Mackenzie.

Tabernacle in the chapel of Christa Sevikas, Pune.
A pomegranate fruit with two fish.
Design: Jyoti Sahi. Photo: Christa Sevikas.

Tabernacle setting in Asirvad chapel, Bangalore. Design: Jyoti Sahi.

the Exodus story and the journey of the prophet Jonah. It was felt these stories were appropriate in reminding the bonded labourers that God is on the side of the oppressed and that one of the important functions of religion is to liberate rather than to enslave people.

In recent years a new regional theologate was built at Sambalpur in the state of Orissa on the eastern coast of India where the Christians are largely Adivasis or Dalits. This chapel has been used as a way of introducing young seminarians to certain basic symbols found in tribal and Dalit traditions and

Chapel of the Regional Seminary, Orissa (above and opposite) with frieze of tribal dancers designed by Wendel D'Cruz
Chapel design: Jyoti Sahi.

their possible re-interpretation in a Christian liturgical context. An example is the symbol of the drum which is central to Adivasi culture and the folk celebrations of Dalits. The form of the drum has been used in different ways, as a decorative feature but also as a structural concept. The drum, which is made of wood hollowed out by fire or of baked clay, has a membrane of leather coming either from a monkey's skin or the skin of a cow. For the tribal, the drum is the divine word, the source of all rhythm and, in a sense, the origin of creation itself. (Sati Clark. Doctoral thesis on "The Drum", Harvard University 1997)

There is also much use of tribal forms of group dancing, both in the liturgy and as a frieze around the church. The offering of the first fruits of the earth, so important in Adivasi festivals like the festival of the Karam Tree, can be related to biblical festivals and the idea of the holy jubilee when the very earth which God has given his people is returned to its source and all relationships are renewed within the overall pattern of the covenant.

This process of rediscovering tribal and Dalit sources of the biblical narrative provides Indian Christians with the possibility for future creative development in the fields of art and architecture. The image of the "tent of meeting" and the use of the triangular form so characteristic of tribal and folk art offers many new ways for the understanding of a Christian interpretation of the Trinity in the Indian cultural context. I have tried on many occasions to use these triangular structures as the basis for my designs because I find them to be dynamic and symbolic of movement and the tribal dance.

As the Church in India increasingly concerns itself with a theology of both creation and liberation, the myths and creation stories of Adivasis and Dalits offer many possibilities for reinterpretation in the light of justice and peace concerns in the Church today. The church building must not only ground a community in its past but should also act as a sign of liberation from former systems of oppression. We can never ignore the fact that the built temple or church has tended to serve an oppressive role as much as a liberative one.

Our task is to find ways in which the structures we build help to free people from negative aspects of institutionalised religion and serve a prophetic function. In reformed Hinduism, as much as in Judeo-Christian religious history, the prophet was critical of the temple cult as serving an oppressive priestly-dominated function in religion. In Orissa, the *mahima* cult, an indigenous neo-Hindu movement of the last century whose great poet was Bhima Bhoi, an Adivasi of the Kond tribe, rejected the temple cult of Lord Jaganath in Puri, saying that the lord of the universe (Jaganath) had now left the precincts of the temple and returned to being a wandering pilgrim amid his suffering people. Here we are reminded of the experience of Moses on Mount Horeb when he discovered Yahweh in the burning bush, a God who had seen, and responded to, the suffering cry of his people.

Towards the end of his life Dr. Abraham Ayrookuzhiel, who had dedicated much of his life to reflection on tribal and Dalit cultures in the context of the Church, expressed a belief that there is a symbiotic relationship between caste and outcaste. Brahmin and *athi-sudra* (or slave), are bound together in a per-

Chapel of the All Indian Catholic University Federation House, Madras.
(above) entrance door with tent-like form.
(below) perforated screen windows (jali) showing the dream of Jacob.

ennial struggle. There are a number of myths which show that God, in the form of Shiva or even Krishna, comes from an outcaste community, representing a counter cultural force within religion. Despite conversion movements, the fact that the majority of Dalits as well as Adivasis have not changed their religion to become either Christian or Muslim, means they have come to realise that finding a new identity does not come simply with rejecting the past or leaving the Hindu fold. (A.K. Coomaraswamy, "The Dance of Shiva", Sagar Pub 1987 and Richard Lannoy, "The Speaking Tree", OUP 1974)

Many leaders of Hindu reformed movements have insisted that Hinduism has to reject its own understanding of caste if it is to rejuvenate itself. The future lies not in the kind of narrow sectarianism which condemns the other, whose religious differences are seen as a threat but rather, in finding new ways of understanding and growing closer together. Conversion as a process should arise from a deep commitment to the forces of growth and transformation. Everyone is in need of conversion. Conversion is not just something which happens at the beginning of a spiritual journey and then, after that, there is no need to change. The whole of life should be a willingness to experience conversion, affirming both continuity and change.

10

Holy Ground

This book is not only about buildings. The basic concern has been to show that the building is an effort to express an underlying theology which has been taking shape slowly in the church.

The context to which we are relating is that of the Indian Church. All the buildings we have seen in this book are situated in India and in some way the form and decoration of these places for worship, prayer or meditation draw their inspiration from elements found in Indian culture. They represent an effort to inculturate the church into the Indian milieu but their significance is not limited to India. An important aspect of this book is to understand what these Asian churches have to say to the churches throughout the world. By its very nature the church is rooted to a particular place which has its own cultural traditions and specific needs but this does not mean that the church is not also universal and catholic in the broadest sense of that term.

When we say that the church building expresses a theology and has to be viewed and understood in the light of that theology, we are implying that the particular form which the Church takes manifests a world view that is not peculiar just to any one particular place or community but addresses issues which are vital for the understanding of the whole church.

So it is important for us to understand how the Indian

Church relates itself to a wider ecclesiology which is shared by the whole church. Further, the local church expresses a vision of mission, which means that the holy place is conceived as something not simply static, or given, but as dynamic and evolving. This way of approaching mission, through the concept of its incarnation in the local church, is a central insight of the second Vatican Council and other church bodies like the World Council of Churches and the Christian Conference of Asia. It is an outcome of a deeper comprehension of what culture represents in terms of systems of meaning, and how this culture relates to the basic values of the gospel. When talking about the church building we are engaged in a process of theologising which does not approach the task of doing theology in the abstract but believes that theologising is in itself an expression of the process of insertion into a lived and concrete reality.

The church building, as we are discussing it in this book, becomes both a metaphor and a context for doing theology in Asia. This means we are laying claims for a wider significance for this effort than is at first apparent. From a first glance we might suppose that these are just very limited, and historically quite marginal, endeavours to realise a theology within a specific situation - that of the Indian subcontinent. But looking deeper, one might suggest that there is much more involved than first meets the eye. For example, these efforts are not concerned merely with adapting traditional styles of architecture for church use but are more profoundly inspired by a new understanding of the relationship of the church to other religions.

The success or failure of these churches involves a whole missiology which does, or does not, accept that other faith systems have something to offer the church. One could argue that the aesthetic success of a given church building is very closely related to the extent to which the theology of those who have commissioned the building has been sufficiently imaginative or not. Thomas Merton argued that the problem of bad art is not that it is merely aesthetically insufficient but that it is even spiritually inadequate. Bad art is bad spirituality - or shall we say bad theology. We may argue that what goes wrong with many church buildings is not just a matter of taste but a fatal loss of what one might call theological nerve. The building falls to pieces not just because its form is not thought through with sufficient artistic feeling but because, finally speaking, its theology is weak. In other words, we are suggesting that theology is not just the gloss, or explanation of an art work, but the very bedrock of its creative feeling and insight.

The churches presented in this book could not be characterised as being aesthetically perfect, any more than the theology which they express in visual forms can be represented as being perfectly realised. The buildings are provisional. They are experiments, with much left to be desired. But they are at least a beginning, in the same way that many churches in the past have been beginnings. It is to be hoped that they do not become ends, tombs, so to say, which unfortunately many churches have degenerated into - the mere shells which have to be discarded if the living, vital principle which is within all creatures is to be set free. Churches should liberate people, not become a dead burden. This means that we need to judge churches and constantly evaluate their continuing significance.

At this point it is essential to distinguish between the church as a living people and the buildings which should edify and give expression to their solidarity.

This book has its limitations. Of necessity we have chosen a particular group of churches, thus focusing on a specific concern. This concern could be articulated as relating to the church's attitude to other religious traditions which characterise the rich tapestry of religious pluralism to be found in India. This focus naturally entails an attitude towards traditions as such, both religious and cultural, especially in India where religions and cultures have been so interwoven. What we have not presented is examples of churches in a modern western style. Questions arising out of the modern cultural situation cannot be overlooked. These have to be addressed, at least in parenthesis, within the framework of an emerging post modernity. An example of this might be glimpsed in the work of the very much respected modern architect, Laurie Baker.

The modern world view which has influenced post independence Indian culture is closely interlinked both with a scientific, technological paradigm which is itself a product of the age of enlightenment - whose concern for progress has been determined by a rejection of the past - and is also contained within an ideology which we might call "secular". It is not within the scope of this book to discuss secularist attitudes which tend to reject the whole idea of the sacred place in itself. But it is important to bear in mind that the aesthetics of an architect like Laurie Baker spring from an affirmation of the holiness of ordinary life and everyday objects, thereby avoiding certain fundamental attitudes to be found in a traditional view of sacred images as being extraordinary and otherworldly.

Throughout this book on Indian churches, running like an undercurrent, there flows an interest in the "counter cultural". Certain modern Indian architects have rejected much of what this book describes. It is important to state their objections to what appears in many ways to be a regression into a sterile past. The so-called inculturated style can easily be seen as just another form of romantic revivalism which fails to recognise the way in which lndian culture has changed, embracing many modern values.

Some years ago, when I was trying to clarify my own thoughts on this issue, I approached the well-known Indian architect Charles Correa to ask him for his reactions to this whole venture into cross-cultural style. He had himself recently been engaged on the building of a very modern church in Bombay which he had designed in collaboration with such leading Indian theologians as his cousin Parmananda Diwakar. In our conversation, Correa presented the rationale behind respecting cultural differences and for that reason not pretending to create a Christian architecture in India from borrowed elements belonging to other religious traditions. At the centre of his argument lay a concept of the sacred building as a sign. He pointed out that a public building, like a church, is not just a functional entity fulfilling certain needs in a community to assemble together for prayer or common celebration but represents that community as a sign of their presence within the society as a whole. If we go to a locality and see a mosque, and recognise it as such, we are able to affirm the presence of Muslims in that area. It is the same with a temple. Not only can we judge from the shape of the temple which particular sect is being represented but we can also gauge how important the community is which has erected the building. Understood in this way, the building represents not only a theology, or cosmology, but it is also a monument to the social diversity which characterises the community in which it has been erected. Similarly understood, the church becomes a focus for the aspirations and self-perception of those who claim themselves to be believing Christians. In this context, it is clear that if the church is built to resemble a mosque or a temple there is a confusion of signs and this ultimately gives rise to a confusion of identity. It could be argued that it is far better to build a church as a modern structure, affirming the liberation from traditional norms and practices of those who worship in it, than to get trapped into a kind of syncretism which ultimately tends to work against cultural plurality rather than for it.

This argument is certainly a very persuasive one and cannot be ignored. But again, given our present situation in India where people of different religions are increasingly stressing their fundamentalist identities and using sacred buildings as the rallying point for aggressive sectarianism, it is also important to demonstrate that the holy place is not meant to be fought over but should provide the opportunity for discovering common ground. In that sense, the holy place is, one might say, primordial and belongs to everybody. The same could be said of a festival. A festival does not simply belong to a Jain community or a Sikh or Hindu or Muslim community, implying that it cannot be celebrated by a Christian. Even basing oneself on the sign value of sacred places and times, one could demonstrate that a sacred place or time should be meant for creating harmony and peace. And the way in which religions have appropriated the sacred in order to make claims of uniqueness is an abuse of the symbolic. Even the cross is not the copyright of Christians, as though it were some kind of trade mark.

The holy and symbolic cannot be reduced to intellectual or religious property rights. The Hindu does not possess the Trimurthi, or the letter OM, any more than the Hindu possesses Sanskrit, or the Christian Latin or Greek. Jesus himself never defined what was supposed to be Christian culture. Christian culture did not arrive with Christ's swaddling clothes. In a sense we could even say that Jesus discarded his native Jewish culture like the shroud when he rose from the dead. The Risen Lord is not limited to any culture in the way that the Jesus of Nazareth was confined to the all too human perspective of a practising Jew. The basilica, the Romanesque Church or later Gothic Cathedral are no more intrinsically Christian than the thought of Plotinus which was adopted by many of the Patristic Fathers. The fact that Christians embraced Greek philosophy does not mean that Greek and Roman philosophy has to provide for ever the framework for systematic Christian thought. In that sense, Advaita is as Christian as anything which Aristotle wrote. So if St. Thomas of Aquinas could use the thought of Aristotle in his Summa Theologica, the Indian Church can also use the Vedanta to express its own faith. This faith is not just the faith of Indians, any more than scholastic theology is only about the faith of Europeans. Assuming as our premise that the church building is an expression of an underlying theology, it is important to stress that the insights which are basic to the temple or mosque are as relevant to Christian images of God as were the forms of Greece and Rome which contributed so much to what we are now calling Christian culture.

In regard to signs, let us look more carefully at what the Christian Church in India has, in fact, signified. For many Indians the church building has represented colonial power. Is this the kind of sign that we want to continue in the minds of Indians? Is it not in fact a counter-sign, the very rejection of all that the Jesus of history stood for when he announced the gospel as a liberation from all oppressive structures? Those who want to get away from all that the church has meant to Indians over many years of colonial domination have tried to find a new style for church building. But styles are not just invented overnight. As Levi Strauss has pointed out, cultures are never "new" in that sense. They are always drawn from the bric-a-brac which past cultures have left behind. Cultures reaassemble, reform, reinterpret what has been common currency for millennia. There is not a single form in sacred art or architecture which has not been borrowed from somewhere else. Although there are some genuine inventions in style, these themselves have developed out of previous forms and have a clear basis in a continuing tradition. Even the form of the Hindu temple can be traced back to Babylonian times. Cultures are forever taking things from each other and redefining symbols. Like a language, images are used in such a way as to give rise to new meanings, new patterns of thought. That is part of the growth of a culture and it is also the growth of a spirituality and religion.

In our effort to understand the significance of a local style, we need to reflect in greater depth on the meaning of tradition itself. Tradition is not just something left over from the past, a kind of deposit representing the accumulation of many cultural memories. It is also something in the present which is lived. In that sense, each one of us is a living representative of the tradition. We are the tradition in so far as the tradition continues to be active through persons and institutions alive today. Here the distinction between tradition and modernity becomes meaningless, because without its present expression a tradition ceases to exist.

The great challenge to modern theology can be compared with the challenge which modern science also faces. It is a challenge to its very terms of reference. What is being challenged is not the truth of the church but the limits of what the church has admitted as truth. The church has defined itself within certain parameters and it is these parameters which are now being questioned. These limits which were set on truth by the organised church possibly derive from some unholy alliance between the church as we have been in the habit of understanding it and the blind spots which characterised the age of so-called "enlightenment". What we are calling truth is itself very much culturally determined.

The patterns of thought taken by logical discursive propositions follow assumptions which lie at the very basis of cultures. According to the culture of the enlightenment, truth becomes equated with reason and that 'reason' is often quite unconscious of its own motivating interests. Every action is determined by certain reasons but these reasons are themselves conditioned by individual or group interests and are, therefore, prone to deep-seated prejudices. Reason becomes like a narrow-tunnel vision, not allowing for any other viewpoint. The universal church needs the truth to be found in other religions, in order to discover its own truth. We need the other in order to reveal our own inner identity, in the same way that we need a mirror in order to see what we look like in the eyes of others. This is the real importance of diversity. Vision has to be many-sided if it is to discover the whole.

There is an old parable, told in many forms in many different cultures, about a man who had a dream. This dream revealed to him that he must go to a very distant land where, on a bridge, a great treasure would be shown to him. On this bridge the man met another dreamer who said: "I too had a dream, in which I was told about a treasure which lies hidden beneath the hearth of a man who lives far away in a land which I have never visited." The first dreamer, recognising in this other dream a description of his own home, rushed back to find the treasure hidden underneath his own hearth. But he had to make this journey to find the other in order to find himself. That is what culture and spirituality are about.

This book is about finding oneself in another culture. And therefore about mission. The church has understood its very nature as mission. Mission is not just something which is done by a group of devoted souls who go to distant lands to bring the truth of the gospel to those who do not know about it.

Mission is something in which everyone is engaged. We come back again to the incarnation and an incarnational theology. Mission is not just something which the church decided to do once Jesus had lived and died. Mission was part of Jesus's own self-consciousness, His way of understanding his relationship to God. This mission, this consciousness, points back to a trinitarian theology which is the very foundation of a creation theology. The Creator sends forth the son into creation to be incarnated in creation. In the same way, the Spirit is sent forth to renew creation. This process of sending forth creative life into creation is the dynamism behind what we are calling mission. Creation is mission. The artist or architect is a part of that creative mission.

This book points to a new understanding of the church as Holy Ground in the sense of sacred space. In this way the church building is not just viewed as a functional structure but as a sacrament in itself. It is the place where certain prayers are offered but in addition it is an expression of that prayer, a gesture of a community's self offering to God. Here we go beyond sectarian differences, even differences of creed, to find a common ground between people of different faiths. In the multi religious context of Indian culture, the Holy Ground needs to express a shared spirituality that is rooted in an experience of God and so is potentially accessible to all. That is why it is so important to rediscover the spiritual dimension of the church building and to make a conscious shift away from an assertion of political or secular power through the building. The Gospel reality addresses not merely an abstract, other-worldly faith, but something incarnated, made visible and tangible. It is in that sense that the liturgy has been spoken of as the "work of God" - a concrete act rising out of a common task. Ultimately it is the spirit that has to show us how to build the church of the future.

Jyoti Sahi

Glossary of Indian Terms

achari...carpenter, master craftsman, traditional architect
adishthan...the base, primal site of temple
adivasi...tribal peoples
ahimsa...non-violence, non-injury, love
ananda...joy, bliss, one of the three qualifications of Brahman
arathi...the circling of oil lamps, flowers, incense etc., in an act of veneration before the divine image.
ashram...a place of refuge, usually a small community centred on a charismatic person
ashrama...stage of life, traditionally four: student, house holder, forest dweller, ascetic
atman...the essence, soul of each individual which is one with the universal spirit
Aum (Om)...the sacred syllable. Regarded as the seed of all mantras or thought forms. Also the three letters can represent Brahma, Vishnu and Shiva
avatar...descent of the divine, the incarnation of Vishnu in animal or human form
bhakta...devotee
bhakti...religious devotion and love toward god
Brahman...the essence of life, the supreme transcendent one, the reality which is the source of all knowing and being
Brahmo-samaj...reform Hindu group founded by Raja Ram Mohan Roy in the nineteenth century in Bengal, rejects elaborate ritual and concerned with social issues
chit...consciousness
Dalit...(lit: pressed or broken into the earth), used for oppressed and outcaste
dharma...duty, righteousness, cosmic order, social and religious observances, that which holds the world together, (modern: religious tradition)

diksha...initiation
farsh...(Arabic lit: the floor), ground made sacred by touching the earth with the forehead at the time of prayer
garbha griha...(lit womb-house), innermost shrine of Hindu temple
ghat...landing place or steps at bank of a river
gopuram...ceremonial entrance, gateway to the temple
guru...spiritual teacher, guide
Harijan...name given by Gandhi to people formerly known as untouchable, (lit: children of God)
Hindutva...Hindu nationalist culture
Kali...the mother Goddess (lit: the black one)
karma...an act and its results which will be manifest in time
khadi...hand-spun, hand-woven cloth revived by Gandhi as a symbol of self-sufficiency and simple living
Krista-bhakti...Christian devotee
Lakshmi...Hindu goddess of good fortune, wife of Vishnu
lila...play, drama, the delight of the god. Ras-lila: a play of delight, a musical drama depicting sacramental circle dances of Krishna
Mahatma...great soul, an honorific title referring to Gandhi, first used by Rabindranath Tagore
makara...mythical semi-aquatic creature, a crocodile with an antelope's head
mandala...the circle or circular diagram depicting the symbolic rendering of the universe
mandapam...temple porch in south India, pillared hall
mandir...temple
mulasthanam...inner sanctuary, holy of holies, the place where god is present
nav-rathri...nine nights of the goddess, each night one aspect of her is venerated and worshipped
Om...see Aum
puja...rites performed in Hindu ceremony
purusha...spirit as opposed to matter
raj...rule, often used for British rule in India 1858-1947
ramayana...Sanskrit epic, story of Rama an incarnation of Vishnu
sadhana...religious discipline, quest, the devotional path

samadhi...profound meditation at tomb of a holy peron
sandhya...sacred time at meeting of light and darkness, particularly dawn and sunset
sanyassi... a person who has renounced all worldy attachments for a life of contemplation and asceticism
Sarnath...a Buddhist site north of Varanasi where Buddha is said to have begun his teaching
sarvodaya...the uplift of all, new social order developed by Gandhi
sat-chit-ananda...being-consciousness-bliss, qualities attributed to the godhead
sat-sang...gathering of holy people
satyagraha...(lit: insisting on the truth), a technique developed by Gandhi for social and political change, based on truth, non-violence and suffering
satyagrahi...one who practices satyagraha
Shiva...the auspicious one, the many powered deity who is both creator and destroyer
Solanki...Chalukya dynasty from Gujarat, originally in the twelfth century, revived in the eighteenth century
stupa...Buddhist monument shaped like a solid dome
swadeshi...belonging to, or made in, one's own country
varna...caste, colour
vasavo...original settler
veda...(lit knowledge) the sacred knowledge incorporated into the the Hindu scriptures as four Vedas
vedanta...(lit: the end of the Vedas), one of the six systems of Hindu philosophy
vihara...Buddhist monastery, usually a cave hall with cells cut into three sides around the central space
vimanam...tower of a temple in south India
Vishnu...the preserver, mainly worshipped by his avatars especially Krishna and Rama
yajna...sacrifice developed by early Aryans

Bibliography

AMALDOSS, Michael, *Becoming Indian-the Process of Inculturation*, Dharmaram Pub. Bangalore 1992.
- *Do Sacraments Change?* T.P.I. Bangalore, 1979.
- *Towards Fullness*, N.B.C.L.C. Bangalore 1991.
- *Life in Freedom - Liberation Theologies in Asia*, Gujarat Sahitya Prakasham, 1997.

BUTLER, John F. *Christian Art in India*, C.L.S., 1986.
- "Christianity in Asia and America", *Iconography of Religion* Vol. XXIV, E.J. Brill, Leiden, 1979.

BHATIA, Gautam, *Laurie Baker: Life, Work, Writings*, Viking Hudco Press, 1991.

COOMARASWAMY, Anand K., *Art and Swadeshi*, Munshiram Manoharal Pubs, 1994.

FLEMING, Daniel Johnson, *Christian Symbols in a World Community*, Union Theological College, Friendship Press NY, 1940.

GUHA-THAKURTA, Tapati, *The Making of a New "Indian" Art: Artists, Aesthetics and Nationalism in Bengal*, Cambridge University Press, 1992.

HARGREAVES Cecil, *25 Indian Churches*, ISPCK Delhi, 1975.

JESUDASAN, Dr Savarirayan, *Ashrams Ancient and Modern*, Sri Ramachandra Press, Vellore, 1937.

KRAMRISCH, Stella, *The Hindu Temple* (Vol I & II), Motilal Banarsidas, 1976.

Liturgical Arts No 1, Nov 1953, "Experiments in Indian Christian Architecture", pub. Liturgical Arts Society.

MACKENZIE, Caroline, "Your Bondage Makes Me Aware of Mine (Reflections on Designing an Indian Christian Temple)" *Faith and Form*, Vol XXVII, Spring 1993.
- "The Cave and the Mountain (Reflections on Designing a Trappist Chapel in South India)", *Church Building* No 36, Manchester Nov/Dec 1995.
- "Cosmic Awareness and Sacred Space: The Integra tion of Feminine Symbolism in Indian Christian Art and Architecture", *Yearbook of the European Society for Women's Theological Research*, Grunwald, Mainz, Feb 1994.

MANIYATHU, Pauly, *Heaven on Earth: A Theology of Liturgical Spacetime in the East Syrian Qurbana*, Mar Thoma Yogam, Rome, 1995.

MALIECKAL, Louis, *Yajna and the Eucharist: An inter-religious approach to the Theology of Sacrifice*, Dharmaram Pubs., Bangalore, 1989.

MENACHERY, George (ed), *The St Thomas Christian Encyclopaedia of India* (Vols I & II), Trichur, Kerala 1982.

NASR, Seyyed Hussain, *Islamic Art and Sprituality*, Oxford University Press 1990.

SRINIVASAN, K.R., *Temples of South India*, National Book Trust 1971.

SYKES, Majorie, *An Indian Tapestry*, William Sessions Ltd, New York 1997.

SAHI J. and MIDDLETON P., *Adisthan: Sacred Space: Indian Christian Ventures*, N.B.C.L.C., 1993.

SAHI J., Kristo Jyoti Chapel, Sambalpur, Orissa, 1993.
- *Window Design for St Mary's Cathedral*, Varanasi, 1992.
- "Designing Spaces: Church Architecture and Windows", *The Eye* Vol 11, No 6, Nov-Dec 1992.
- *Stepping Stones: Reflections on the Theology of Indian Christian Culture*, A.T.C. Bangalore, 1986.

TAKENAKA, Masao, *Christian Art in Asia*, C.C.A., 1975.
- *The Place Where God Dwells: An Introduction to Church Architecture in Asia*, CCA and ACAA, Pace Pub. 1995.

TAYLOR, Richard, *Christian Ashrams as a Style of Mission in India*, I.R.M., July 1974.

THAPAR, Romila, *The Past and Prejudice*, National Book Trust, 1977.
- *Exile and Kingdom*, Bangalore Mythic Society, 1978.

TOMBEUR, James, *Led by God's Hand*, Thirumalai Ashram, 1990.

VANDANA, Mataji (ed), *Christian Ashrams: A Movement with a Future?* ISPCK, Delhi, 1993.

VOLWAHSEN, Andreas, *Living Architecture: Indian*, Oxford and IBH Pub., Fribourg, 1964.

Index

(photographs in bold type)

Abhishiktananda, Swami, 134
Acharis, 24, 67
Adivasis - see tribals
Akbar, 60
Amaldoss, Fr Michael, 12, 123, 136
Amalorpavadas, Fr D.S., 12, 118, 134
Ambedkar Dr B.R., 141f
Aurobindo, 93
ashrams, 13, 91-110, 118
ashram, Names :
 -Aikya Alayam, Madras, 92, **171**
 -Anand Matha, Kerala, **132**, 133
 -Anjali, Mysore, 106
 -Art Ashram, Bangalore, 11f
 -Aurobindo, Pondicherry, 77, 93
 -Bharat, Begharia, 92
 -Christa Prema Seva, Pune, 105, 108, 136, **172**
 -Christava, Kerala, **101**
 -Christu Kula, Jolarpet, **104**, 105f
 -Edaikodu, **95**
 -Gyan, Bombay, 91
 -Kurisumala, Alampundi, 11
 -Maitri Sagar, Kolar Gold Fields, 169, **170**
 -Mathridam, Varanasi, **121**, 122
 -Sameeksha, Kalandy, 119
 -Santineketan, Birbhum, 92, 98, **99**
 -Shantivanam, **83**, 105, 134
 -Snehasadan, 92, 155
 -Yesu, Kamanahalli, **126**
Asian Christian Art Association, 7, 12
Asoka, 82
Ayrookuzhiel, Dr Abraham, 148, 176
Azariah, Bishop, 141f

Babri Masjid, 12
Baker, Laurie, 11, 101, 113f, 145, 155
baptismal font, 32
Barbosa, Fr Francis, 92
Benares - see Varanasi
Bengal School of Art, 54
Bhagavad Gita. 76, 118
Bhoi Bhima, 176
Binyon, Lawrence, 58
Bodewig, Fr, 149
Brahmo Samaj, 92
Buddhism, 23
Buddhist architecture, 96
Butler, Rev John, 58f, 68

Cambridge Mission, 62
cathedrals, 40, 139-158
Cathedral, Names
 -Agra, old cathedral, 59, 60
 -Dornakal Cathedral, 142, **143**, 148
 -Kohima Cathedral, Nagaland, 166
 -Palai Cathedral, Kerala, **29**, **32, 33**

195

-St John the Baptist, Tiruvalla, 145, **146, 147**, 155
- St Mary's Cathedral, Varanasi, **150**, 151f
Celestine, Sr., 169
Chandy, Acharya, 103
Christian Conference of Asia, 180
Church Missionary Society, 45
Church, Names
- Almut Memorial Church, Mehrauli, Delhi, 70, **71**, **72**
- Bettiah Church, Patna, **62**
- Bom Jesu, Goa, 85
- Cheriapalli, Kottayam, 25
- Turkman Gate, Delhi, 65, **66**
- Isubath Mandir, Gujarat, 164
- Kaduthuruthy, Kottayam, **27**, 30
- Kalupara Syrian, **24**
- Kuruvilangad, **26**, 29
- Melpalai, Tamilnadu, **88**
- Mokameh Shrine, Patna, **59**, 60, 77
- Muttattur, Arcot, **158**
- Nallayanpuram, Tamilnadu, **89**
- Parakunnu, Tamilnadu, 11
- Puthupally Syrian, Kottayam **39**
- St Andrew's, Calcutta, 43, **44**
- St Andrew's, Madras, 43, 44
- St John the Baptist, Gwalior, 73, **74**
- St Helens, Patna, 61, 63
- St Mary's Votive, Madras, 144, 156,**157**
- St Thomas, Delhi, 152, **154**
- Salvacao, Bombay, 155
- Uteshwari Shrine, Gujarat, 166f, **167**, 168

- Velliapalai, Kottayam, 27, **31**
colonialism, 37-52, 75f
Coomaraswamy, A., 55, 56, 67
Coonan cross, 28
Coore, A, 62, 65f
Corbusier, Le, 68, 155
Correa, Charles, 155f, 182

da Fonseca, Angelo, 107
da Gama Vasco, 22
Dalits, 50, 93, 141f, 159-178
Daniels, Rev John, 134f
Dann, Reginald, 63, 65f
Davis J.R., 145
De Foucauld, Charles, 126, 132
Dev, Fr Anil, 122
doorstep, 129
doorway, 129
D'Souza, Fr Claude, 169
D'Souza, Bishop Patrick, 149f
Duff, Alexander, 68

Elwin Verrier, 105
Emerson, William, 58
Eucharist, 34, 134f
Evangelism, 13, 75f, 122f, 161

floor space (farsh) 25
Forrester-Paton, Ernest, 107

Galdos, Fr I., 164f
Gandhi, M.K., Mahatma, 42, 63, 76, 93f, 141f, 155
globalisation, 14, 20, 43
Gothic architecture, 41, 48
gopuram, **28**,**104**
Grant, Sr Sara, 108, 136
Griffiths, Fr Bede, 11, 80f, 135
Guha, Thakurta Tapati, 54
Gurukul Lutheran Theological College, 137

196

Hargreaves, Cecil, 65
Havell E.B., 55, 58, 65f
Heras, Fr Henry, 63
Hinduism, 23, 53f, 76f, 141f, 164
Hindu architecture, 25, 50, 63, 79, 107, 129
Holy Roman Empire, 38

incarnation, 21
inculturation, 15, 43, 129
Indian Missionary Society, 122, 149
Indo-Saracenic, 58, 62
inter-faith dialogue, 123
Irudayam, Fr Ignatius, 134
Irwin, John, 26
Islamic architecture, 25, **57**, 67, 132, 142, 152f

Jacobites, 28
Jesudasan, Dr S., 105f
Jesuits, 28

Khanna, Kishen, 79f
Kramrisch, Prof Stella, 25

Lash, Fr Bill, 108
Lebbe, Fr Vincent, 87
Lederle, Fr Matthew, 12, 155
Lethaby, W.R., 58
liturgy, 31
Lutyens, E.L., 68, 153

Mackenzie, Caroline, 169f
Malenfant Mgr F., 149
mandala, 34, 127, 152
mandapam (pillared hall), **47, 98, 113, 158**
martyrium, 133f
Mazoomdar, P.C., 76
Menezes, Archbishop, 42, 43

Menon, Krishna, 152f
missionary movement, 75-90
missionaries, 22, 43f, 80f
Missionary Sisters, 149
modernisation, 13
Monchanin, Fr Jules, 81f, 105, 134
Mosque, 23f, 70
Munda, Ram Dayal, 160
National Biblical, Catechetical and Liturgical Centre, 11, 118, **119, 120**
Nehru, Jawaharlal, 68, 69
Nepal, 23, 60
Noreen, Sis Barbara, 107

Orientalism, 53-74, 78

Padmanabhapuram Palace, 87
Painadath, Fr Sebastian, 117
Panikkar, Raimoundo, 79, 123
Pereira, Teotonio, 37
Pieris, Fr Aloysius, 135, 140
pilgrimage, 86
Portugese, 28, 37f, **39**, 75
prayer rooms, Name
 - Ashirvad Chapel, Bangalore, 126, **138, 173**
 - Bentinck Girls School, 69, **70**
 - Mekiad Chapel of Trappist Sisters, **131**
 - Women's Christian College, Madras **64**
Proksh, Fr George, 91

Qutb Mosque, 70, 153

Rajagopalchariar. C.R., 141
Ramakrishna, 60, 77, 92
Ramana, Maharishi, 77, 86
Ramayana, 92f

197

Ram Mohan Roy, 76
Regional Theologates, Names
- Kristo Jyoti Mahavidyaloyo, Orissa, 115, 116, 117, **174, 175**
- Sambalpur, **115, 116**
- Sameeksha, Kerala, 117
- Tamilnad Theological Seminary, Madras, **113,114**
roof, 24f, **101, 147, 168**
Roy, Jamini, 79

sacrament, 17
sacred space, 16, 131, 179-187
Singh, Sadhu Sundar, 78
Sen, Keshab Chandra, 77f, 92
Shankara Acharya, 23, 53, 82, 117
Society of Friends (Quakers), 63, 90
Society of the Auxiliaries of Mission, 87
Spain, 37f
Sykes, Majorie, 63f, 90
Syrian Church, 16, 19-36, 41, 45, 128, 141
Syro-Malabar Church, 28, 46
Symbols
- baptism, 135
- cave, 16, 79, 131f
- cross, 26f
- dance, 175
- drum, **116**, 175
- flagstaff, 25f
- home, 128f,
- lamp, 29, 35
- light, 22, 118, 131
- oil, 29
- lotus, 33
- monster, 33
- time, 129
- tree of life, 26, 127

- womb, 48, 79
Tagore, Debendranath, 76, 92
Tagore, Rabindranath, 42, 63, 76, 80, 92, 98, 133
Takenaka, Masao, 7, 8
Taylor, Dr Richard, 92
Temple architecture, 23, 30f
Temples, 50
Temples, Name
- Mylapore, **28**
- Kaladi village, **49**
- Kottayam village, **49**
- Shiva Temple, Pondicherry, **110**
- Tulsimanasa Mandir, Varanasi, 112
Temple of the Tooth, 84
Thapar, Romila, 38,39, 50, 54, 94
theology, 20, 82, 162, 180
theologates, 111-124
Tombeur, James, 11, 87
Tribals (avidasis), 50, 93, 95, 159-178
trinity, 78

Upadhyay, Brahmabandhab,77f

Varanasi, 12, 118, 123, 149f, 163
Vatican Council II, 145, 180
Vivekananda, Swami, 76f

Wesley, Frank, 165
Wickremesinghe, Lakshman, 77, 82f
Women's Christian College, Madras, 64, 65
World Councl iof Churches, 180
World Missionary Conf'ce, 142

Xavier, Francis, **167**
yoga, 127

> Holy Ground is one of many books
> of the Asian Christian Art Association
> dealing with Asian Christian art and architecture

The Place Where God Dwells
An Introduction to
Church Architecture in Asia
Edited: Masao Takenaka
112 pages, 50 distinctively Asian churches

The Bible Through Asian Eyes
Edited: Masao Takenaka and Ron O'Grady

Over 100 full colour art works from 18 Asian countries
together with meditations by Asian writers
A visual delight

Frank Wesley
Exploring Faith With a Brush
Author: Naomi Wray

One of India and Asia's great Christian artists
224 pages contain his best-loved works

Available from Pace Publishing,
Box 15774, Auckland, New Zealand
Fax: 64-9 817 35 74
Email: pace@iconz.co.nz

The Asian Christian Art Association
was formed in 1978 to encourage Christian artists in
Asia by giving them a forum to exchange ideas and
promote their work.

The ACAA
publishes books, photos, and videos
provides scholarships for emerging artists
organises and mounts exhibitions of art
holds periodic Asia-wide conferences for artists.

The ACAA
promotes its work through *Image* magazine
This quarterly magazine contains beautiful
colour photographs by Asian artists
and has information and news
of the Association.

The ACAA
can be contacted at the following address:

c/- Kansai Seminar House
Takenouchi-cho, Ichijoji
Sakyo-ku, Kyoto 606
JAPAN